They Flew to Glory

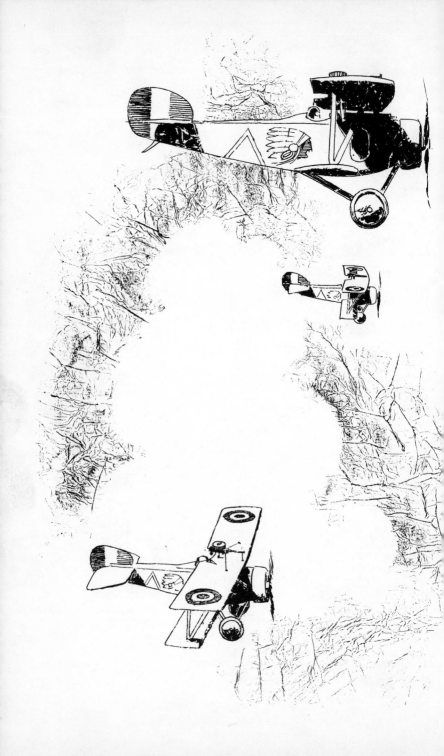

THEY FLEW TO GLORY:
The Story of the Lafayette Flying Corps

by Robert Sidney Bowen

Illustrated by Bernard Case

Lothrop, Lee & Shepard Co., Inc.
New York

Chapter

ONE

When World War I began on July 28, 1914, there was no such thing as a military combat airplane. The warring nations did have airplanes, but they were used only for observation flights or to land and pick up spies behind enemy lines. High military men of the time scorned the possibilities of the airplane as a military weapon. They insisted that an army required troops and cavalry and artillery to win a war—not "those unreliable flimsy contraptions!"

As a consequence, the eighteen countries involved in World War I at the outset possessed a collective total of only about five hundred airplanes. Of that number all were of civilian design, almost half were in repair shops, and not a single one was equipped to fight in the air.

Although man had been flying airplanes since 1903, it was not until 1910 that the armed forces of the great powers had been persuaded to officially accept the airplane as a weapon of war. The British Royal Flying Corps, the French Flying Service, the German Air Force, and one or two other military aviation services were established in the years that followed. But these fledgling air services were not set up as separate military units.

They were classed simply as temporary adjuncts to the regular army, and were completely under the orders of army commanders.

The pilots were given the rank of corporal or sergeant, while the regular army-trained men who flew with them as observers were all commissioned officers. Very little money was allotted to the aviation units, and they remained small in scope throughout the prewar years. For example, when the British Royal Flying Corps was sent to France in the first days of World War I, it consisted of exactly thirty-eight airplanes. And if the United States had entered the war at that time, it would have done so with only *three* military airplanes!

There were three different types of planes in wide use at the beginning of the war: two-seater tractor airplanes with the engine in front, two-seater pusher airplanes with the engine behind, and a few single-seater airplanes. To be truthful, most of the planes were, as the generals said, somewhat "unreliable flimsy contraptions" and more often than not they were underpowered. It was a feat just to get one of those early military planes off the ground, and another feat to land it safely. In spite of the handicaps pilots and observers did a magnificent job serving as "the eyes of the armies," even in the war's early days. They flew long patrols observing enemy troop movements and spotting the effectiveness of artillery fire, and also made daring forays into enemy territory to land or pick up spies.

At first the pilots flew unarmed, but it wasn't long before the commanding generals on both sides saw the possibilities of aerial combat: if your "eyes" could put out the enemy's "eyes," then the enemy would be blind.

The name and nationality of the airman who fired the first shot in aerial warfare was never recorded, but the story most often told by airmen of the time concerned a German pilot and observer and a Russian pilot and observer.

6

Their airfields were located opposite each other on the Russian front, and every day each pair would fly an observation patrol behind the other's lines. They would pass going out on patrol and when coming back, and it wasn't long before they started waving as they flew by. Then one day the Russian pilot and observer did not wave. It was probably because a different pilot and observer were in the Russian plane that day, and they were unaware of the custom. Apparently, though, the German pilot and observer failed to think of that possibility. Instead they considered the Russians' failing to wave as an insult and resolved to do something about it.

The next day the German observer took a shotgun along on his patrol, and when he flew by the familiar Russian plane he let go with both barrels. Of course the shotgun slugs didn't even come close to the Russian plane, but its pilot and observer were enraged by the attempted attack. The following day the Russian observer took a rifle along, and as the two pilots flew their planes by each other the two observers started blazing away. Both missed their targets, but they had nevertheless set the basic pattern for the deadly art of aerial warfare.

Soon all observers were going aloft with a pistol or rifle or shotgun, and blasting away at any enemy airplane encountered on patrol. Although there is no record of any early airplanes being shot down by this method, there were some instances of aircraft being forced to earth by enemy planes without benefit of aerial gunfire.

One day three British Royal Flying Corps pilots sighted a German two-seater some three thousand feet below them. The British leader signaled the other two and all three went diving down on the German plane. They came so close before they pulled out of their dives that the German pilot panicked and headed for the ground. The three British pilots dived on him again and again, and eventually the German had no more air-

space for maneuverability. His plane hit the ground and was smashed to bits.

Another instance was that of a British pilot in a single-seater who harried a German down to the ground from a height of several thousand feet. Fortunately for the German he was able to land his plane safely, but he was so unnerved by the experience that he jumped out of the plane and ran away. The British pilot promptly landed in the same field, hurried over to the German plane, and set it on fire. Then he took off and flew safely back to his own airfield.

A third story of how airplanes were downed in those early months of the war is almost too fantastic to believe, but it actually happened. The method used was credited to French airmen, and was called the Bag of Bricks technique. A pilot and his observer would carry a small bag of bricks with them on patrol. When an enemy airplane was sighted, the pilot would get as close to it as he could and his observer would then hurl the bag of bricks at the spinning disk of the enemy airplane's propeller. Good aim would result in the wooden propeller being shattered, and the pilot forced to glide down and land in the nearest field. It is a matter of record that two German airplanes were downed by the Bag of Bricks method, but the practice failed far more often than it succeeded and was soon abandoned.

In a short time pistols, rifles, shotguns, and bags of bricks began to be replaced with machine guns. At first the effectiveness of the aerial machine gun was limited. On a pusher type of airplane the gun was mounted on the observer's nacelle, or enclosed shelter, at the front end of the fuselage. It could be fired up or down at anything in front or on either side of the airplane, but not at anything behind it.

On the tractor type of plane the machine gun was mounted atop the observer's cockpit behind the pilot. Unlike the gun on the pusher plane, it could be fired up or down at anything to the rear of the plane, as well as on either side—but it could not be used against a target in front of the airplane. On both types of airplane only one half of the possible attack area could be covered by the observer's aerial machine gun. Also, on many of those early two-seater aircraft the additional weight of the machine gun reduced the flying capability of the plane. The extra weight often made it impossible for the plane to attain the altitude needed to observe enemy troop movements or the effect of artillery fire, and sometimes it even kept the plane from reaching the altitude of enemy aircraft.

The early single-seater airplane had the machine gun mounted on the center of the top wing, high enough for the bullets to clear the tips of the whirling propeller. The pilot fired the gun by a cord attached to the trigger. However, the machine gun's ammunition drum could hold only a limited number of bullets and had to be replaced frequently. To do so, the pilot had to stand halfway up in the cockpit, holding the joystick between his knees, and use both hands to take off the empty ammunition drum and fit on a full one. It was a tricky procedure and quite often the wash of air from the propeller would blow the full drum right out of the pilot's hands. Often, too, he would run out of ammunition just as he had an enemy airplane in his sights, and before he could reload the machine gun the enemy plane would be gone.

The one big advantage of the single-seater airplane armed with a machine gun mounted on the top wing was that the pilot could point his airplane in any direction and fire his machine gun at the same time. A number of airplanes were shot down by the early single-seaters, but not nearly enough to give one side an advantage in aerial warfare over the other.

What was needed was a single-seater fighter plane with enough *dependable* fire power to protect its own slow two-seater observation planes from all types of enemy aircraft, no

10

matter from what direction they attacked. This problem was solved early in 1915 when it became possible for a single-seater pilot to aim his airplane and fire his machine gun bullets *between the spinning blades of his propeller.*

The man who conceived the idea was a Frenchman named Roland Garros, who was to become known as "The Father of Air Dueling." Long before World War I Garros had made a name for himself on both sides of the Atlantic as a daring and skillful aviator. Between 1909 and 1914 he won almost every airplane flying contest of importance in both Europe and the United States.

At the outbreak of war Garros was on vacation in Germany, and because of his flying skill the Germans wanted to take him into custody and intern him for the duration. Fortunately for Garros, he learned that France and Germany were at war before the German police could get to the hotel where he was staying. Leaving all his baggage behind, he fled to Switzerland, and from there made his way into France.

As soon as he reached Paris, Garros offered his services to the French Flying Service. He was accepted immediately and assigned with other notable French civilian pilots to Escadrille No. 23. For the next five months he flew at the front, skillfully performing all the duties required of a pilot in those early days of the war. He flew trained observers far behind the German lines, and did his full share of the highly dangerous work of landing and picking up French spies in enemy territory.

Garros devised a means of attaching small bombs to his airplane, to be released by pulling a lever in the cockpit. Then he decided, early in 1915, to try and find some way to fire machine gun bullets between the spinning blades of his propeller. If he could solve this problem, he would be able to mount the gun on the engine's hood directly in front of his cockpit where he could reach it easily and reload it quickly. He went to work building and trying out various devices which he thought might function satisfactorily, and eventually settled on one that was crude in design—but which did the job.

He placed the machine gun on the hood of his single-seater's engine with the muzzle pointed at a spot about one third the distance up from the hub of the propeller to the tip of the blade. Then he made two wedge-shaped strips of steel that were about as long as half the length of a propeller blade. He fastened these strips to the near face of each propeller blade so that they extended from the boss, or shaft, halfway up the blade. The purpose of the strips was to deflect any bullets that happened to hit the propeller blades instead of passing between them. Garros had them extend above and below the place on the blade at which the fixed machine gun was pointed, in case vibration caused the gun to shoot a little high or low. He fired the machine gun by means of a wire attached to the trigger that led back to his cockpit.

When he tested his invention, Garros was pleased to find that the 7 per cent of bullets that did hit the propeller's blades were all deflected off by the strips of wedge-shaped steel. At the same time he was aware of three serious drawbacks. Most serious was the possibility that the deflected bullets might ricochet back and hit a vital part of the plane, or even the pilot himself. The strips of steel attached to the blades also reduced the propeller's efficiency, and they put an added strain on the airplane's engine as well. But the advantages of the device seemed to outweigh the disadvantages, and in late March of 1915 Garros decided to test his invention in actual aerial combat.

Taking off from his squadron's airfield in his Nieuport plane, he flew across to the German side of the lines and began patrolling up and down the front in search of enemy aircraft. For a while he was alone in the air, but eventually he sighted three German two-seater observation planes headed for the French lines. Since he had the advantage of altitude, he nosed down slightly to gain additional speed and took after his prey.

The Germans saw the diving plane, of course, and were able to tell that it was a French Nieuport. But as there wasn't any machine gun mounted on the top wing, they naturally believed it to be unarmed and made no attempt to head away. Too late they realized their mistake. Garros quickly closed in on them; lining up his sights on the middle plane of the trio, he opened fire. The pilot and observer were instantly killed, and their plane went hurtling earthward out of control. By then the other Germans had recovered from their shock and flew full out for safety. But Garros was not yet finished. He went streaking in at a second German two-seater to set it on fire and send it spinning down to destruction, leaving behind a long trail of oily black smoke.

While Garros was scoring his second victory, the pilot of the third German plane was able to scoot away to the safety of his airfield far behind the lines. According to German reports, when he and his observer reported what had happened, their squadron mates at first refused to believe them. Eventually, though, the surviving pilot and observer convinced them that the impossible had really taken place. A French Nieuport pilot had downed the two other airplanes by shooting a machine gun through the spinning blades of his propeller. Word of Garros' mysterious aerial machine gun spread quickly throughout the German Air Force and plunged it into a state of confusion.

During the next three weeks Garros shot down four more enemy airplanes. His phenomenal success with his invention resulted in an order being issued by the French Air Service high command that all single-seater aircraft be equipped with the device. The French Government decorated Garros for his splendid work, and he became France's air hero of the hour.

13

Unfortunately, Roland Garros' days of glory were soon to come to an end.

On April 19, 1915, he once more took off from his airfield alone in search of German aircraft. As on every patrol Garros flew, his little Nieuport was fitted with some small bombs to drop on any military target he might pass over. That particular day the air behind the German lines was empty of enemy aircraft. Eventually Garros' supply of fuel began to run low and he was forced to turn around and head back toward the French side of the lines.

While still some miles inside German-controlled air, and at an altitude of a good ten thousand feet, Garros suddenly spotted a poorly camouflaged enemy ammunition dump. Since he still had his small bombs, he decided he might as well inflict some damage on the Germans so that his patrol wouldn't be a total loss. He switched off his engine and went down in a long silent glide toward the ammunition dump.

The Germans on the ground didn't hear or see his tiny airplane approaching until it was too late to do anything about it. Garros was almost on top of them when he released his bombs and, at the same time, switched on his engine. The bombs hit a corner of the ammunition dump and did considerable damage, but Garros was too preoccupied to take a good look. His engine would not start!

Either the spark plugs had been fouled by the long powerless glide, or else the rotary engine was flooded with oil. Whichever the case, the engine refused to start despite all Garros' efforts to get it going. With the engine dead, he knew his only hope was to land in the nearest field and set fire to the Nieuport before German ground troops could reach him.

Some German soldiers saw him gliding down, however, and rushed out onto the field to surround the Nieuport with rifles ready as it rolled to a stop. Garros had no chance whatsoever to destroy the plane and its valuable military secret. He was quickly taken prisoner; after the usual interrogation by German Intelligence, he was sent to a prisoner-of-war camp deep inside the country. During the next three years he tried several times to escape, but was recaptured on the first two attempts. Not until January of 1918, when he tried a third time, did he succeed in making his way back to the Allied side. From then until the war's end he once again flew and fought in the sky for France.

It was tragic that Roland Garros, so soon after perfecting his vital invention, should have been the very one to deliver it into the hands of the enemy. His captured Nieuport was immediately turned over to the German Air Force for examination, and technical experts quickly discovered the secret that had been giving the Germans such concern. A Dutchman named Anthony Fokker, who was later to design the deadly German Fokker fighter plane, was called in to study Garros' invention and devise something similar for use on German airplanes.

Within a few days Fokker designed and built a device that was far superior to Garros' crude invention. And in England, at almost the same time, British experts were perfecting a mechanism that would prove to be every bit as effective and efficient as Fokker's. Soon afterward every country in the war had a workable device of its own to permit a plane's machine gun to shoot between the spinning blades of the propeller.

In the months and years that followed the capture of Roland Garros in his little Nieuport on April 19, 1915, many pilots on both sides of the war were to become great air aces. And many flying units were to cover themselves with glory in the relentless battle for control of war skies.

Perhaps the most famous of all these units was the Lafayette Flying Corps, a gallant group of Americans who volunteered to fly and fight for France.

Chapter
TWO

The creation of the Lafayette Flying Corps was inspired by an American pilot who never flew with that famous air fighting unit. In fact, when the Corps came into being on March 14, 1916, he was living out his eighth month in a German prisoner-of-war camp.

The pilot's name was James J. Bach. He was born of wealthy American parents residing in Paris and had lived most of his life in France. He grew up there, attended French schools, and graduated from a French university with an engineering degree. As a young boy he had spent an occasional summer visiting the United States with his parents, but when he was old enough to travel alone he used all of his vacations to roam around Europe.

When World War I broke out, Jimmy Bach was working for an engineering company in Italy. On hearing the news he resigned his position and returned to France to volunteer to fight for the country he had come to regard almost as his homeland. When he got off the train in Paris he went into the first recruiting office he came to and offered his services. To his amazement they were flatly rejected. The recruiting officer explained that there was a French law prohibiting anyone of foreign birth from serving in the regular French army. But he added that Bach could enlist in the French Foreign Legion if he wanted to fight for France.

The French Foreign Legion has been demobilized for some years now, but in its day it was one of the most colorful fighting forces on the face of the earth. It was a severely disciplined, hard-fighting military unit composed of volunteers from every walk of life, and from every corner of the globe. In its ranks could be found soldiers of fortune, adventurers, mercenaries, scholars, men of lost honor, and escaped criminals who ranged from petty thieves to ruthless murderers. The Legion accepted anyone who could pass a simple physical examination. What a man's real name was, where he was from, and what he had done before he enlisted were of absolutely no interest to the recruiting officers. For many years the Foreign Legion fought only in the North African colonies, but when World War I started it was brought to France to fight alongside the regular French army.

Jimmy Bach applied for enlistment in the French Foreign Legion on August 24, 1914, and was accepted. After a short training period he was sent to the Marne front to serve in the trenches. Early in December, Bach was standing guard duty in a muddy trench, keeping a sharp lookout on the German trenches some two hundred yards away across No Man's Land. It was a cold day, but for a rare change there was a clear blue sky flooded with sunshine. Suddenly Bach saw two airplanes flying toward each other—a French plane from his side of the lines and a German plane from the enemy side. He had sighted airplanes wheeling about in the sky before, but never had he seen two flying so low and obviously heading toward each other to engage in aerial combat.

Although Bach knew nothing about airplanes, he could at

least tell that both aircraft were two-seaters. They were flying at the same altitude when suddenly the French pilot pulled his plane up sharply. The German started to follow him, but by then the Frenchman had reached the top of his zoom. In a flash he cartwheeled over on one wing and went diving down on the German. Seconds later Jimmy Bach heard the savage rattle of the Frenchman's aerial machine gun. A moment afterward the German two-seater seemed to stagger in the air, and then lurch over on its back. With black smoke streaming out behind, it hurtled down and crashed in flames not a quarter of a mile from where Bach stood.

As he watched the air battle's grim conclusion, Bach found himself yearning to join the fight for the skies, instead of being confined to a muddy trench. The more he thought about it later, the more he resolved to somehow obtain his transfer from the Foreign Legion infantry to the French Flying Service.

When his tour of guard duty was finished, Bach went straight to his company captain and put in a request for the transfer. The captain thought he was mad to want to risk his neck in an airplane and tried to dissuade him, but Bach only became more determined. Eventually the captain reluctantly promised to do all he could to obtain the transfer. On December 10, 1914, Jimmy Bach received it, together with his orders to report to the French flying school at Pau.

Upon reaching Pau he found that there were far more flying students than there were airplanes for them to fly. As a result he had to wait his turn, and it was not until March, 1915, that he began his flight instruction. On July 4 he completed his training on the two-seater Caudron biplane. And on August 29 he was assigned to French Escadrille No. 38.

Escadrille No. 38 flew the two-seater Morane Saulnier high wing monoplane, or the Morane Parasol as it was more often called. Bach's observer was a Lieutenant Giroux, and together

18

they made several uneventful observation flights over enemy territory. Then one day they spotted a German two-seater in their sector of the sky. However, since they were on an important observation mission, they ignored the enemy and continued with their job—until the German observer started shooting at them from long range.

Only a pair of bullets punched holes in the Morane Parasol's fabric-covered wing, but that was two too many for Jimmy Bach. He cut short the observation flight and set off in pursuit of the German two-seater, which was now headed toward its home airfield.

Bach already had the advantage of altitude and he shoved the plane's nose down to gain all the additional speed possible. The Morane Parasol was not built for such hard flying and every wing and strut began to vibrate from excess strain. Lieutenant Giroux screamed at Bach to abandon the pursuit before their plane came apart in mid-air. But Jimmy ignored his pleas and continued roaring on down until he caught up with the German two-seater a few miles behind its own lines.

Closing in on it, he took aim and fired the machine gun mounted atop the Morane Parasol's high wing. Almost immediately the German observer slumped over in his cockpit, and the airplane went skidding off to one side. Bach chased after it and took aim at the pilot and engine. At that critical moment his gun jammed.

When he was unable to clear the gun stoppage, Jimmy yelled back at Lieutenant Giroux, who had a gun fitted to his cockpit, "I'll try to get in close underneath, so you can use your gun!"

Bach dived the Morane Parasol for extra speed, and then hauled it around and up underneath the belly of the German two-seater. Lieutenant Giroux raked it with machine gun fire from propeller to tail, and in seconds it burst into flame. As it fell out of the sky, Jimmy Bach leveled off his plane gently and

20

eased it around toward the French lines several miles away. The air battle was over, but the danger was just beginning.

The frail little Morane Parasol had taken a terrific beating from the wild maneuvering. The wings and fuselage were vibrating violently, and the controls were so sluggish Bach had to use every bit of his piloting skill to keep the plane in the air. In addition, the overstrained engine sounded like a rock crusher. At any moment he knew it might quit and force them to land on German ground where they were almost certain to be taken prisoner. But the fear that plagued him most as he flew westward was the possibility of an attack by other German planes before they reached the safety of the French lines. The battered Morane Parasol just wouldn't be able to take another air battle. If it didn't come apart by itself, it would undoubtedly be shot down.

But luck was flying with Jimmy Bach and Lieutenant Giroux that afternoon. Although they sighted other German planes, none was near enough to make an attack. Eventually Bach nursed the plane all the way back to a safe landing on their home airfield. A little later he and Lieutenant Giroux learned that some French soldiers in an advanced outpost had witnessed the air flight and seen the German two-seater fall to earth in flames. Because of their testimony Bach was officially credited with shooting the enemy plane down.

That German two-seater proved to be Bach's only air victory, but it was enough to win him the rank of corporal and a place in air-war history as the first American to shoot down an enemy airplane. Quite possibly he would have gone on to become the first American air ace—a winner of five air victories—if his luck hadn't run out on him. Or perhaps it would be more fitting to say that because of his daring, and his willingness to risk his life for his comrades, Jimmy Bach practically forced his luck to run out on him.

It happened on September 23, 1915. Bach and another pilot, Sergeant Mangeot, were summoned that morning to the office of their squadron commander. When they reported, the commander instructed them to land two French spies behind the German lines. It was just another routine mission for them, since they had both made several spy flights before. Only half a mission actually, because they would not be making a second flight to pick up the spies. The two French agents dressed in civilian clothes were both experienced in the dangerous task of committing sabotage behind the enemy lines and evading capture. On this trip they were to dynamite a railroad line the Germans had been using to transport troops and supplies to the fighting front, then make their own way back through the lines to the French side.

Just before take-off, Bach and Sergeant Mangeot checked over last-minute details with their passengers. The two spies were both familiar with the area of German-held ground in which they would operate, and they pinpointed the exact spot on the map where they wanted to be landed. They assured Bach and Sergeant Mangeot that there were no German troops within miles of the spot. The landing should present no problems whatsoever.

Bach led the way into the air with his spy and Sergeant Mangeot followed him up with the other spy. As soon as they had sufficient altitude they headed out across No Man's Land and on into German-controlled air. Because of the great importance of the mission they avoided all contact with enemy aircraft. Whenever they spotted a German plane they climbed into the safety of some clouds and kept on going.

After a little over an hour's flight Bach spotted the field where they were to land. He signaled to Sergeant Mangeot and started gliding down while his eyes searched below for any possible sign of German soldiers. There was no evidence of enemy troops, but when he was low enough for a good look at the field itself he saw something that made him groan with dismay. The field was almost entirely covered with scrub growth and small trees! Not knowing anything about airplanes, it probably hadn't even occurred to the two spies that what they thought was a perfect spot to touch ground could well be a hideous nightmare for two pilots trying to land their frail aircraft.

Bach's immediate reaction was to abandon any attempt to land the spies in the growth-choked field. The only alternative was to fly around and find some other field where he and Sergeant Mangeot would at least stand a halfway decent chance of landing without cracking up, and of getting safely off into the air again.

He soon realized, however, that there wasn't any suitable field in the vicinity. The entire area was composed of rugged terrain and the growth-covered field was the only possible landing spot. Besides, time was of utmost importance, leaving Bach and Mangeot no choice but to try and land in the hazardous field.

After circling the field several times and studying it from all sides, Bach signaled to Mangeot that he was going down. Luck was with him—at least for the moment. After missing a couple of small trees by a whisker, he touched solid ground and brought the Parasol to a stop. His spy jumped quickly out of the rear cockpit and went racing across the field to disappear in some bordering woods. Bach didn't even see him go. He was too busy twisting around in the seat to watch Sergeant Mangeot slide down and also make a safe landing.

Just as soon as Mangeot's spy joined the other one in the woods, the two pilots set themselves to the task of getting their planes back into the air. Bach tried it first. He gunned the engine full out and after bouncing over the rough ground for an alarming distance, and missing small trees by inches, he finally managed to lift the frail Morane Parasol clear and go climbing up into the air.

He gave a joyful shout of relief as he banked and watched Sergeant Mangeot start his take-off run. But seconds later he cried out in alarm. Mangeot was just on the point of lifting his plane clear of the ground when his right wing caught on some tall bushes. It sent the little Morane Parasol skidding crazily to the right, and before Sergeant Mangeot could do anything to counteract the movement, the monoplane flipped over on its back. For a moment fear caught at Bach's throat. Then he saw Mangeot crawl out from under the overturned plane and wave his hands to indicate he was uninjured. The French pilot then pointed toward the French lines and shook his clasped hands above his head in a gesture of good luck.

Jimmy Bach started to wave an acknowledgment of Mangeot's gesture, but checked himself. He knew he could fly back to the airfield and report the successful landing of the two spies, and Sergeant Mangeot's crack-up, and no one would think any the less of him. In fact, it was the sensible thing to do—but he just couldn't bring himself to do it. He had landed in the field once, and perhaps if he pushed his luck a little he'd get away with it a second time and save Sergeant Mangeot.

He banked his Parasol around and flew to the down-wind end of the field. Then he throttled his engine and glided down to make a second successful landing on the bumpy patch of ground. As the plane jolted to a stop, Sergeant Mangeot ran over to it and scrambled into the observer's cockpit. No sooner was he settled safely than Bach opened up his throttle and began his second tricky take-off.

For several moments it looked as if he were going to make it, but then, as he was lifting the little Morane Parasol clear of the ground, the left wing tip grazed a tree. Actually it just barely touched the tree, but it was enough to swing the airplane around

24

to the left and send it straight toward a whole clump of small trees. Bach tried desperately to rudder the Parasol away from them, but there wasn't enough room. The airplane plowed full out into the trees and was completely demolished.

Amazingly, Bach and Mangeot suffered only minor scratches, and were able to scramble out of the wreckage and run for the protection of the nearby woods. But once they were hidden among the trees the two pilots knew they didn't dare move. Any attempt to make their way back to the French lines in broad daylight would be doomed to failure. Their flying clothes would give them away to the first German who saw them, not to mention the French uniforms they wore underneath. Yet it was equally dangerous for them *not* to move away from the woods. It was entirely possible they had been seen circling the field, and at that moment German soldiers might be on their way to investigate. When no one was found in either of the crashed airplanes, the entire area would undoubtedly be searched.

To be captured and taken prisoner of war was an unpleasant enough prospect. But if the Germans found out they had landed spies, they would never see the inside of a prisoner-of-war camp; they would be stood against the nearest wall and shot just as if they were spies themselves.

After talking the situation over at length in whispers, Bach and Mangeot decided the lesser of the two evils would be to remain where they were until dark. The decision made, they settled down to wait, and as luck would have it not a single person appeared to investigate the two crashes during those seemingly endless hours. When darkness finally came the two pilots stole out of the woods and started cross-country toward the west. Some three hours and twelve miles later their journey came to an abrupt end when, confused by the pitch blackness, they stumbled into the arms of a German patrol and were captured.

Under armed escort they were taken to German Headquarters at Laon and questioned for hours. The Germans strongly suspected they had landed spies because there were only two of them, while both the crashed planes, which had been discovered, were two-seaters. However, the spies had not been captured and the Germans had no proof.

Jimmy Bach and Sergeant Mangeot stuck doggedly to their story that they had both been on patrol without observers, and when one of them had had a forced landing and crashed, the other had also crashed when he tried to rescue him. In an effort to trip them up, the German Intelligence officers asked all sorts of trick questions, but Bach and Mangeot managed to avoid every pitfall. Still not believing their story, the Germans gave them a military trial, but it resulted in a "no verdict" judgment.

Ten days later they had to stand a second military trial for landing spies. By then, though, Jimmy Bach had been able to get hold of some of his personal funds through the Swiss Red Cross and he hired a Berlin lawyer to defend them. At the second trial he and Mangeot were found not guilty, and they were sent to a prisoner-of-war camp deep inside Germany.

Bach tried several times to escape from the camp, but he was recaptured each time. He remained a prisoner of war until the Armistice was signed on November 11, 1918, after which he was finally released and returned to France.

The military flying career of Jimmy Bach was unfortunately brief. But this brave and resourceful man would always be remembered as the first American to shoot down an enemy plane, and he would serve as the inspiration for many other Americans to fly and fight for France.

Chapter
THREE

In the first month of World War I a total of twenty-nine Americans enlisted in the French Foreign Legion. Jimmy Bach was the first of them to transfer to the French Flying Service, but he was soon followed by William Thaw, of Pittsburgh, Pennsylvania. Bill Thaw played an important part in forming the Lafayette Flying Corps, and was the only one of its seven original members still on active flying duty when hostilities ended.

Thaw was a big man with thick dark hair, black eyes, and a walrus mustache. He had learned to fly a Curtiss hydroplane in the United States, and was on a pleasure trip through Europe when World War I erupted. Having visited France often and become very fond of the country, he cut short his travels and went to Paris to enlist in the French Flying Service. However, like Jimmy Bach, he ran up against the French law forbidding any foreigner to enlist in France's regular armed forces.

The reason for that law, incidentally, was the French fear that foreign espionage agents might filter into the ranks of their regular fighting forces—especially into the French Flying Service. An enemy spy on the ground was dangerous enough, but in an airplane he could obtain unlimited military information for the country he was actually serving.

The French had good reason to be suspicious, judging by the following incident which occurred early in the war when a man with forged American papers succeeded in enlisting in the French Flying Service. How he was ever allowed to enlist still remains a mystery, but he was accepted and sent to the French flying school at Pau. There he took his flight training, but when he was about to be breveted, or commissioned, and sent to a squadron at the front, he suddenly disappeared. Some two months later he turned up in the United States posing as a French pilot on leave. Through newspaper interviews, and magazine articles which he wrote, he spread stories that were most damaging to France in the eyes of millions of neutral Americans. Later it was discovered that the same man had sold valuable French military information to the German Embassy in Washington, D.C.

As a result of this and other incidents, the French tightened up their screening of everyone seeking to enlist in the French Flying Service. Even after the law was finally rescinded in 1915, French military authorities maintained a constant secret surveillance over all aviation enlistees of foreign birth. There were several known cases where two French Secret Service agents, posing as Flying Service enlistees, bunked on either side of a foreign-born flight student in training at a flying school. One or the other was the "suspect's" constant companion until his loyalty to France was proved beyond all doubt.

Bill Thaw wasn't aware of any of this when he tried to enlist in the Flying Service and he was amazed when his application was refused. The fact that he already knew how to fly didn't make the slightest bit of difference. Like Jimmy Bach before him, Thaw enlisted instead in the Foreign Legion. He received his basic training at Rouen and Toulouse, and on October

16, 1914, after a six-day march to the Marne front, he started his active service in the French trenches.

Late in October Thaw's infantry company was pulled out of the lines and sent to the rear for a rest. While there, he and two other Americans obtained permission and transportation to visit the airfield of a French squadron located some thirty miles from the rest camp.

The squadron's commanding officer, Captain de Gorges, was honored by the visit of three Americans wearing his country's uniform, and he personally conducted them on a tour of the airfield and its facilities. Thaw and his two friends were excited by what they saw, and before the visit was over all three were pleading with Captain de Gorges to help them obtain transfers from the Foreign Legion to the French Flying Service. The captain promised to do all he could, and two months later his efforts were successful. But *only* for Thaw's two friends. They received their orders of transfer, while Thaw, the only one who actually knew how to fly, did not receive any orders at all.

Angry and upset over this disappointing turn of events, Thaw obtained leave from his infantry company's commander and walked the thirty miles to the same French flying field. When he told Captain de Gorges his story, the French officer was dumbfounded since he had understood that all three were to receive their transfer. He assured Thaw he would do everything he could to straighten out the mix-up, and he was as good as his word. On the day before Christmas, Bill Thaw's transfer papers came through. And to his great joy he was not being sent to a French flying school for training, but was being assigned to French Escadrille No. 6 at the front!

When he reported to Escadrille No. 6, though, Thaw's joy took a sharp nose dive. He found out that he had not been sent to the squadron to serve as a pilot, but rather as an observer.

Thaw's first impulse, upon hearing the news, was to go to his commanding officer and register a vigorous complaint, coupled with a request that he either be given the duties of a pilot or else be sent to a flying school where he could be breveted a pilot. But on second thought he decided against any such action. He'd had too hard a time getting into the French Flying Service in the first place to run the risk now of angering his superiors and possibly being returned to the Foreign Legion.

Thaw decided to keep his feeling of dissatisfaction to himself and concentrate on performing his duties as an aerial observer. He made a number of patrols over German territory with his pilot, but each new flight served only to increase his desire to become a war pilot himself. In time he did start pleading with his superiors to be sent to a flying school where he could obtain a pilot's commission. He even claimed he could fly any type of aircraft, when actually the only one he had ever flown was the American Curtiss hydroplane.

At last his efforts were successful. On February 1, 1915, Thaw said good-by to his flying mates at Escadrille No. 6 and left for the military flying school at Saint-Cyr. But as soon as he arrived he found himself in a bad spot—one he had brought on himself. His claims of being able to fly all types of aircraft had preceded him! As soon as he was settled in his quarters, the commanding officer of the school ordered him to take up a French two-seater Caudron observation plane and give a demonstration of his piloting ability. It was an order Thaw was to long remember, for not only had he never flown a Caudron, he had never even seen one before!

However, he felt there was nothing he could do about the embarrassing situation except to try and fly the Caudron. If he refused, he was sure he'd become the laughing stock of the school, and have a black mark against him before he even started flight training. So, with an unspoken prayer he climbed

into the Caudron. While he warmed up the engine he anxiously studied the instrument panel. He took his time taxiing out into take-off position so as to have a chance to feel the controls and the aircraft's reaction to them. But the moment came when he knew he couldn't stall any longer. He swung the Caudron around into the wind, gave the engine full throttle, and took off.

Bill Thaw was later to say that beginner's luck had certainly been with him that day, but his successful flight was due to a lot more than just luck. It was his natural flying ability that really saved the situation for him. He remembered everything he had learned while flying a Curtiss hydroplane, and applied that knowledge and a little something extra to flying the Caudron. When he landed, the commanding officer commended him for the way he had handled the demonstration flight. The ticklish crisis was over.

Thaw progressed rapidly in his training at Saint-Cyr, and the day when he would be breveted a pilot seemed to be drawing nearer and nearer. Unfortunately, though, another disappointment lay ahead. Thaw was breveted, but to his disgust he was not assigned to a French squadron at the front. His superiors decided that because of his experience as an observer with Escadrille No. 6 he would be of more value for the moment serving as a pilot for French army officers who were in training at Saint-Cyr to become expert aerial observers. Much to his displeasure, but unable to do anything about it, Thaw took up his new duties. Then on March 20, when he was in Paris on a two-day leave, he met a fellow American by the name of Norman Prince, who was to suggest an unexpected way out of his dilemma.

To Norman Prince must go the credit for being the first man to conceive the idea of forming an all-American air squadron to fly and fight under French colors. Prince came from Prides Crossing, Massachusetts, and was the son of very wealthy parents. Although rather small in size, he was a powerfully built man with blond hair, blue eyes, and on occasion a mustache. He was a fine horseman and polo player, and had spent many summers in Europe, particularly in France. He spoke French fluently, and like Bill Thaw, he had warm feelings for the country and its people. He, too, happened to be in France that summer of 1914 when World War I started, and decided almost immediately that he wanted to fight under the tricolor flag.

Since he had become interested in aviation in America the year before, Prince at once investigated the possibilities of enlisting in the French Flying Service. He learned, of course, that the existing French law ruled out both the Flying Service and the army. He had the choice of enlisting in the French Foreign Legion or in a recently formed volunteer ambulance-driving unit known as the American Field Service. Neither of those interested him, so he decided to try a different way to get into the French Flying Service. He would go back to the United States and learn to fly, then return to France and offer his services to the French Flying Service as a licensed pilot.

Prince took the next boat back to the United States and with a friend, Frazier Curtis, enrolled in the Burgess Flying School at Marblehead, Massachusetts. It was while he was taking his flight training at the Burgess school that Prince thought of the idea of an all-American squadron in the French Flying Service. When he talked it over with Frazier Curtis, his friend was all in favor of the idea. But first Curtis wanted to find out if he could enlist in the British Royal Naval Air Service, as it appealed to him more than any other aviation unit of the fighting countries. If he could not get into the RNAS he would then join Prince in France and enlist with him in the French Flying Service—and help him try to organize an all-American French air squadron.

In early January, 1915, both Prince and Curtis graduated from the Burgess Flying School and received their pilot's licenses. Prince sailed for France to try and enlist in the French Flying Service, and Curtis sailed at the same time for England to see about joining the British Royal Naval Air Service.

When Curtis arrived in England he found out that his enlistment application would be accepted, *but* he would have to forfeit his American citizenship. Later that British ruling was revoked and foreigners could enlist in the British armed forces "for the duration of the war" without losing their citizenship. But the old law was still in force when Curtis tried to enlist in the RNAS, so he changed his mind about flying for England and crossed over to France to join Norman Prince.

In the meantime Prince had arrived in France and been accepted by the French Flying Service. By then the French law about foreign-birth enlistments had been rescinded, and he had no trouble at all. He was sent to the Pau school to take his training on French military airplanes, but the school was full and he had to wait five weeks before he could start. However, Prince had not forgotten his dream of an all-American squadron flying for France, and he spent those five weeks trying to get the ball rolling. Frazier Curtis had joined him at Pau by this time, and he lent his help in trying to interest several influential people in the idea.

Among those they approached were two prominent Americans living in France, Robert W. Bliss and Robert Chandler, who arranged interviews for them with important members of the French Ministry of War. Another influential man who came to their aid was Dr. Edmund L. Gros, head of the American Field Service. Two others, Jarousses de Sillac, a prominent French Government official, and Colonel Barres, the chief of Aeronautics in the French Army, also gave their support to the idea of an all-American squadron. So did William K. Vanderbilt, the American multimillionaire, and several others.

Indeed it was quite an imposing list of Americans and Frenchmen who sought the French Government's permission to form an all-American squadron that would fly and fight under the French flag. But it was to be many months before Norman Prince's dream became a reality, for like all governments, the French Government was hampered by red tape, and few of those in high positions were willing or able to attempt to cut through it. Several of the high-ranking officials approached were very much in favor of the idea, but just as many were completely against it, and for various reasons. The principal obstacle, though, was not of French origin: the United States Government was trying to maintain a position of absolute neutrality in the conflict raging in Europe, and frowned on *any* American fighting for a foreign nation.

However, Norman Prince continued to press for an all-American squadron, and when he met Bill Thaw on leave in Paris he enlisted his help. With French permission to form such a squadron seemingly as remote as ever, Prince had thought up a new approach. He wanted Thaw's help in getting the French authorities to order all Americans taking flight training at various French schools to assemble at the Pau flying school. It was Prince's hope that once they were all together at Pau, there would be a much better chance of forming an all-American squadron to be sent to the front.

Bill Thaw wasn't too enthusiastic about the idea, though. Not because he didn't want to see an all-American squadron established—he was all for it. But it so happened that his own tour of duty at the Saint-Cyr airfield was ending and he was due to be sent at last to a French squadron at the front. Naturally Thaw didn't want to risk losing that assignment, with its promise of front-line action, in order to simply stay behind at Pau on the chance that an American squadron might be formed at some future date.

Soon after his meeting with Prince, however, Thaw received

orders to report not to the front, but to the Pau airfield where he would join the other Americans and take more flight training. Angry at this change in plans, Thaw instead of reporting stormed into the offices of the French Ministry of War in Paris and demanded to be sent at once to join a French air squadron at the front. His demand was granted and on March 26, 1915, he joined French Escadrille No. 42 stationed on the Nancy front. It proved to be a smart move on Thaw's part, for as things turned out, having all American volunteers take their flight training at Pau did not result in the formation of an all-American squadron. When the Americans were breveted pilots, they were merely assigned to various French squadrons at the front. Prince himself was sent to French Escadrille No. 108.

However, once Bill Thaw was settled in French Escadrille No. 42, he did start giving active support to Prince's dream of an all-American squadron. In December of 1915 he and Prince, together with Elliot Cowdin, another American pilot flying for France, went on an extended leave to the United States in a dramatic attempt to win their countrymen's backing for the project.

That trip proved to be one of the most astonishing adventures any of the three pilots ever experienced. When they first arrived in their homeland they were praised and feted, but soon they became the objects of harsh and bitter criticism. Those who had honored them were Americans who believed in the Allied cause, and looked upon the trio wearing French Flying Service uniforms as splendid examples of what Americans could do against a ruthless enemy which was menacing the democracies of Western Europe.

In 1915, however, there was also a good-sized segment of German sympathizers living in the United States. They were the thousands of German-born people who had emigrated to America years before and become naturalized citizens, but who still held the Fatherland dear to their hearts. These people loudly denounced Thaw, Prince, and Cowdin as adventure-seeking violators of America's strict stand of neutrality in the European war. They even petitioned the authorities in Washington, D.C., to have the trio arrested and interned for the duration.

Washington turned down the petition, and when their leave was up, Thaw, Prince, and Cowdin returned to France and their flying duties at the front. Their trip home had not in any way changed Washington's official stand of strict neutrality, but it had publicized coast to coast what some Americans were doing to help the Allied cause. And this publicity inspired many other Americans to go to Europe and fight with the French and British armies before the United States finally entered the war in 1917.

When the three fliers arrived back in France they found the all-American squadron idea still bogged down by red tape. A committee of prominent Americans and Frenchmen, with Jarousses de Sillac as chairman, had been formed to help speed up operations, but it had not succeeded in making much headway. Those high in French government and military circles were still divided as to the advisability of such a squadron. Half argued that France would gain tremendous favorable publicity throughout the world by having an air squadron made up of volunteer American pilots. But the other half argued just as vehemently that it would be a foolhardy undertaking because the United States Government frowned on any American fighting for a foreign power.

Meanwhile the war went on. Bill Thaw continued to fly at the front with his French Caudron squadron. Norman Prince was transferred from his French Voisin squadron to the military flying school at Le Bourget for training on the single-seater Nieuport pursuit biplane. Many other Americans who had transferred from the Foreign Legion or the American Field Service, or who had enlisted directly in the French Flying Service, were receiving their flight training at the Pau flying school.

In January, 1916, after almost a year and a half of effort by many people, it looked as if Norman Prince's dream of an all-American squadron flying for France would forever remain just a dream. But its realization was a mere two months away.

Chapter
FOUR

The Lafayette Flying Corps had its official beginning on March 14, 1916, when Jarousses de Sillac received word that the French Government had accepted the proposal of his committee. An all-American air squadron was to be organized at once and dispatched to the French front as soon as possible.

The work of organizing the squadron went into high gear immediately, and on April 17 Norman Prince gave a celebration dinner in Paris for a number of American pilots, some of whom were already serving with French squadrons. The highlight of the evening came when Prince stood up to read the official pilot roster of the new squadron which was to be known as *Escadrille Américaine* N. 124. The N stood for the Nieuport pursuit plane the squadron would fly. The seven original members of the *Escadrille Américaine* were:

William Thaw, Pittsburgh, Pennsylvania
Norman Prince, Prides Crossing, Massachusetts
Elliot Cowdin, New York, New York
Kiffin Rockwell, Asheville, North Carolina
Victor Chapman, New York, New York
Bert Hall, Bowling Green, Kentucky
James McConnell, Carthage, North Carolina

The pilots on the official roster were ordered to report to a French airfield as Luxeuil, located near the eastern boundary of France. As soon as the dinner was over, Norman Prince, Victor Chapman, Kiffin Rockwell, and James McConnell left Paris by train for Luxeuil. Two days later they were joined by William Thaw, Elliot Cowdin, and Bert Hall. On April 20 *Escadrille Américaine* N. 124 was officially declared on duty at the front.

The commanding officer of the new squadron was Capt. Georges Thénault, and his adjutant was Lt. Alfred de Laage de Meux. When the American pilots arrived at the Luxeuil railroad station the two French officers were there to meet them with squadron automobiles. That was a pleasant surprise; before they had always had to walk from the railroad station to an airfield. Another unexpected surprise was the very comfortable rooms assigned them in a villa next to the famous Luxeuil Baths. And to top things off, they were informed that they would mess with their commanding officers in the best hotel in town. The French Government may have taken almost a year and a half to reach a decision about the squadron, but now that it was a reality, apparently nothing was too good for the American volunteer pilots.

What pleased the pilots most, however, was the airfield and its equipment. Everything the French had provided for them was brand new: the fleet of Nieuport pursuit planes with fixed aerial machine guns that fired through the spinning propellers; the hangars, the squadron buildings, and the rest tents where they could relax between patrols; the repair shop, all the motor transport, and many other items necessary to a front-line squadron.

To keep everything in perfect operating order there was a corps of experts in their respective fields—airplane riggers and engine fitters; armorers, motorcyclists, and telephone men; also wireless operators, ambulance drivers, medical men, and squadron clerks.

How the pilots felt about the base as a whole was very aptly expressed by one of them in a letter back home. He wrote: "Everything is so grand I almost feel as though I'm visiting a summer resort instead of being stationed at a wartime flying field!"

Last but not least of the surprises the Americans received upon arrival at Luxeuil airfield was promotion for all of them. Bill Thaw, who had seen the most service at the front, was elevated from sergeant to lieutenant. Norman Prince, Elliot Cowdin, and Bert Hall were promoted from corporal to sergeant. And Kiffin Rockwell, James McConnell, and Victor Chapman were given the rank of corporal.

However, promotions, brand-new equipment, and a corps of experts to keep it operating didn't blind the Americans to the fact that they had come to Luxeuil for one reason only—to help fight a war. If any of them did forget that purpose for a time, they were given a grim reminder of it just a few days after their arrival.

The American pilots shared the Luxeuil airfield with a French bombardment squadron, and Captain Thénault took them over to its headquarters and introduced them to the commander, Captain Happe. The bombardment squadron commander greeted each of the Americans warmly. Then he pointed to eight little boxes on a nearby table and said, "They each contain a *Croix de Guerre* for the families of the eight men we lost on our last trip over the German lines. It is good to know that you are now here to help us; there are many enemy airplanes in this sector of the front."

The Americans solemnly assured Captain Happe that they would do their best, but it was to be a while before they saw any combat flying action. Captain Thénault was a seasoned veteran of aerial warfare. He had no intention of letting those under his command fly over German territory until he felt they were ready—not even those pilots who had already seen service with a front-line squadron. His goal was an efficient and effective flying *unit*.

Once the new pilots were settled at Luxeuil, Captain Thénault had them familiarize themselves thoroughly with the flying characteristics of their Nieuport pursuit planes. All flying was done over or around the field. Under no circumstances was a pilot to go anywhere near the front lines. The pilots also practiced formation flying, and aerial gunnery on ground targets close by the airfield. When the Americans weren't flying, Captain Thénault took them on motor trips through the nearby Vosges Mountains so they would be well acquainted with various landmarks which could serve as guides to the location of their airfield. Captain Thénault also took advantage of the trips to point out certain places where the pilots could make a safe landing in the event their engines quit before they reached the field.

For three weeks the Americans were drilled daily in the techniques of flying at the front. During their off hours the seven pilots spent much time discussing an important problem— the choice of an official insignia to designate their squadron. Dozens of different ideas were proposed and considered before they finally settled on a painting of the head of an American Indian wearing a war bonnet of red, white, and blue feathers. One of the squadron's mechanics, who was also an artist, painted the colorful insignia on either side of the fuselage of each of the Nieuports. Soon after the last of the insignias had been finished, Captain Thénault announced that the squadron would make its first patrol over the German lines on May 14. Take-off was scheduled for six o'clock in the morning.

At a briefing before take-off, Captain Thénault carefully

pointed out on a map the patrol route they would fly. He also told the pilots that they were not to engage any enemy aircraft in combat unless forced to do so. It was to be strictly a surveillance patrol with the major emphasis put on maintaining flight formation and direction.

Once the captain led them aloft, though, his pilots seemed promptly to forget the various landmarks that had been pointed out to them on the map during the briefing. No doubt first-flight nervousness, and having to concentrate on keeping formation, had a lot to do with their errors. But from take-off until they were all safely back on the ground again, Captain Thénault had his hands full keeping his fledglings herded together and headed in the right direction.

One pilot in particular had a rough time of it on that first patrol of *Escadrille Américaine* over the German lines. He was James McConnell, who never before had flown higher than seven thousand feet, and who had experienced trouble keeping other airplanes in sight ever since his flying school days.

To make sure he wouldn't lose sight of his flying mates this time, McConnell immediately climbed above the formation and went trailing along behind it.

This might have solved the problem for him if it hadn't been for two factors which he failed to take into account. There was a ground mist that morning which blotted out a lot of the landmarks below, and also the sky was filled with clouds. As a result, McConnell was flying serenely along when suddenly he realized that there was no formation of Nieuports just ahead and below his position—there was only a layer of clouds!

Not only was he alone in the sky, but he was also hopelessly lost. None of the few landmarks he was able to see below looked familiar. Ten or more minutes passed as McConnell, his anxiety growing, wandered lost through the sky. When he had almost given up hope of rejoining the squadron, he flew

43

by a patch of clouds and there below him was the formation of Nieuports.

McConnell made sure he stuck close to the other planes as Captain Thénault led the way across No Man's Land into German-held air. The formation had just finished climbing to an altitude of thirteen thousand feet when it received its baptism of German antiaircraft fire. Fortunately none of the ugly gray bursts came close; as a matter of fact, the antiaircraft fire wasn't half as unpleasant for the American pilots as the bitter cold air at thirteen thousand feet. They were all chilled to the bone despite the fur-lined flying suits they wore. The rarefied air at that high altitude also made breathing most uncomfortable until the pilots learned how to take long deep breaths.

That first raggedly flown patrol, however, was by no means a failure for the pilots, nor a disappointment to Captain Thénault. The Americans felt it had been both interesting and instructive. And on evaluating their performance, Captain Thénault decided that they had made no more mistakes than was usual for pursuit pilot beginners. The fact that they had not sighted a single enemy airplane was no great disappointment to the pilots, either. They all knew that combat with the Germans in the high sky would come soon enough.

It did just four days later on May 18 when Kiffin Rockwell became the first member of *Escadrille Américaine* to shoot down a German plane in aerial combat.

Kiffin Rockwell, who came from Asheville, North Carolina, was believed to have been the first American citizen to offer his services to the French Government in World War I. Three days *before* France declared war on Germany Rockwell wrote a letter from his North Carolina home to the French consul at New Orleans, Louisiana. In it he said that "in case of actual war between France and Germany" he wished to volunteer to fight for France, a country which he greatly admired and one which he would be proud to serve on the battlefield.

In a letter of reply the French consul wrote that his office could not receive enlistments, and that Rockwell would have to go to France if he wanted to join the French armed forces. When the war was only half a month old, Rockwell sailed for France, and the day after he landed he enlisted in the French Foreign Legion. He served in the ranks of the Legion for a year, and on many occasions proved himself to be a brave and resourceful soldier. On May 9, 1915, he was severely wounded in the thigh during a victorious assault by the Legion on the German-held town of La Targette. By the time he was discharged from the hospital and had rejoined his Legion company in the front-line trenches, Rockwell had decided to apply for a transfer to the French Flying Service.

His transfer application was accepted and on September 2, 1915, he was sent to the French flying school at Avord. From Avord he went to Pau and then to the school at Le Bourget, where on October 21 he was breveted a pilot on the Maurice Farman two-seater observation plane. From that date until he became one of the seven original pilots of *Escadrille Américaine* he helped train French officer observers, and learned to fly single-seater aircraft.

On that memorable May 18, 1916, when Kiffin Rockwell scored his first aerial victory, he took off from the Luxeuil airfield to check out some repairs on his engine, and perhaps make a "little tour around." Finding that the engine was functioning to his satisfaction, he flew over to the German side of the lines near the city of Thann. Scarcely had he entered German airspace when his engine started to act up on him. Fearing it might quit and force him to land on enemy ground, he immediately banked and headed back toward the Luxeuil airfield.

As he was crossing over to the French side of the lines once more he suddenly spotted a German observation plane some two thousand feet below him. It was the first German plane he had ever encountered in the air, and although his engine was missing badly he couldn't resist the urge to challenge it. He immediately dropped the nose of his Nieuport and went diving down on the German two-seater.

The German pilot had apparently spotted the French Nieuport at the same time, for as soon as Rockwell started his dive the German put his two-seater's nose down in a desperate effort to break away and get back behind his own lines. While the German pilot dived full out, his observer fired furiously at the Nieuport piling down from high air. Rockwell ignored the continuous blasts of bullets ripping by his plane and kept on going down.

He withheld his fire until he was no more than twenty-five yards from the German plane. Then, lining it up in his sights, he opened fire. Only a few bullets left his gun before he had to veer away or else risk flying head on into the German plane. The instant Rockwell was clear he looked back, just in time to see the German observer slump over in his cockpit. Seconds later he saw the pilot also crumple in his cockpit. For a few seconds the German two-seater continued its long dive toward safety. Then suddenly it fell over on one wing, and with oily black smoke trailing out behind, it went plunging down to crash in flames just inside the German lines.

Once the enemy plane had crashed, Rockwell banked away quickly and headed for the Luxeuil airfield. Because of his wild power dive on the German, his engine was now rumbling like a stone crusher and threatening to blow itself apart in the air. Twice it seemed about to quit cold, but both times it somehow managed to keep running and Rockwell was able to make a safe landing on the Luxeuil field. Not long after he had landed, word came through to the squadron that French soldiers in the advanced lines had witnessed the air battle and seen the Ger-

man two-seater crash in flames. Thus was *Escadrille Américaine's* first air victory officially confirmed and credited to Kiffin Rockwell.

The most amazing thing about the victory came to light later when the squadron armorer examined Rockwell's Lewis machine gun. He found that only four bullets had been fired! It was Rockwell's first patrol alone, the first time he had met a German plane, and the first time he had fired his aerial machine gun in battle. And all he had needed was just four shots!

That was the first of several air victories Kiffin Rockwell was to score, but only it and one other downed German plane were officially credited to him. He didn't receive credit for his other victories because they were scored too far behind the German lines to be witnessed by any friendly eyes.

In World War I hundreds of German planes were shot down and destroyed for which no Allied pilot got credit. To receive official credit the victory had to be witnessed by at least two people on the ground, or two pilots in the air, or two Allied balloon observers.

Airmen did not wear parachutes in the First World War, so there were never any chutes floating earthward to give evidence of an aircraft having been shot out of action. The occupants of a doomed airplane had to ride their plane down to destruction on the ground—or, as happened many times, throw themselves out of a burning airplane to escape the excruciating pain of death by fire.

Oftentimes, too, a badly shot-up German plane would manage to limp back to its home field only to crash on landing. That was an Allied air victory, but it could not be officially credited to any pilot, since only the Germans witnessed the climax. And they released no information on such losses.

It was generally agreed among Allied pilots in World War I that a good 70 per cent of shot-down German planes crashed on the enemy side of the lines. The reason for this was that the Germans rarely carried the air war to the Allied side. They seldom penetrated deep into Allied air, and almost never alone. Also, they almost always flew in numbers and would not attack unless theirs was the superior force.

Allied pilots employed very different tactics. Alone or in force they went hunting German planes deep into enemy air and gave battle wherever they found them, regardless of whether they were outnumbered or not. On many, many occasions a lone Allied pilot scored an air victory, but too far behind the German lines to be witnessed and confirmed by his own people.

Kiffin Rockwell's first air victory was officially confirmed, however, and was the cause for great celebration by the pilots of *Escadrille Américaine*. During the next two weeks they flew three and four patrols a day over the German lines. When they were not escorting the French bombers stationed at their field, they would roam the skies alone in search of German aircraft. No more air victories were scored during those two weeks, but the pilots' intensive training under Captain Thénault began to show itself. They became an efficient air fighting unit that could more than hold its own against anything the Germans had to offer. Recognition of that fact by the French high command came early in June.

The squadron was ordered to Bar-le-Duc on the Verdun front. There the most furious fighting was taking place, and the seven Americans were thrilled at being sent to the hottest theater of the war. However, the night before they left Luxeuil an incident occurred which saddened them and made them even more grimly determined to prove their worth at Verdun.

Shortly before midnight a large force of German bombers flew over the Luxeuil airfield and saturated it with bombs. Several mechanics were killed and there was considerable equipment damage. Many buildings and half of the field's transport were destroyed, but by some miracle not a single Nieuport plane was touched. Night flying and fighting by pursuit planes was unheard of in those days, so the American pilots were helpless to take off and give chase to the enemy bombers. They and all the other squadron personnel could only sweat it out in bomb shelters and slit trenches until the Germans had flown away.

The next day the Americans flew their Nieuports to the Bar-le-Duc field. When they arrived they discovered they would be flying in fast company. Stationed at an airfield adjoining theirs were France's two crack pursuit squadrons. One was Escadrille N. 3, the famous *Cigognes* (Storks), of which the great Capt. Georges Guynemer was a member. At this time Guynemer was already the air idol of all France. He continued to rack up air victories, and by September 11, 1917, a little more than a year later, he had shot down the impressive total of fifty-four German planes. On that day he took off alone on a patrol over the German lines and was never seen or heard from again.

The other top-ranking pursuit squadron was Escadrille N. 65, in which the famous Lt. Charles Nungesser served as a pilot. Nungesser was to shoot down a total of forty-five German airplanes, and survive the war. But death in an airplane was to be his eventual lot. In the spring of 1927 he and his navigator, Lieutenant Coli, took off from the French coast in an attempt to fly the Atlantic nonstop to New York City. A ship some eight hundred miles off the coast of France reported sighting their big airplane flying high in a westerly direction, but that was the last that was ever heard of them. They were the first two of several pilots who died attempting to fly the Atlantic nonstop, before Lindbergh made his historic New York to Paris nonstop solo flight on May 20–21, 1927.

All the pilots of the two crack French pursuit squadrons were most friendly to the American pilots who had come to join them in the air battle against the Germans. They went out of their way to make the newcomers comfortable, and help them get ready for the hard flying days to come. Lieutenant Nungesser, in particular, showed a keen interest in the American pilots. He frequently visited them and talked about the various types of German planes they could expect to meet on that front and how best to maneuver against them.

On one such occasion one of the American pilots asked him to explain more fully a certain aerial maneuver to be used against the Germans. In reply Nungesser said that rather than try to tell them in words he would attempt to show them by an actual demonstration in the air. He obtained Captain Thénault's permission to borrow one of the American squadron's Nieuports, and with three of the American pilots he took off and flew over the German lines in search of an enemy plane.

A short time later the pilots sighted a German two-seater observation plane. While the three Americans sat upstairs watching, Nungesser demonstrated how to attack a two-seater from below and behind so that the enemy plane's observer could not fire his gun. Nungesser shot down the two-seater, and then, having proved his point, he led the Americans back to the Bar-le-Duc airfield where he resumed his talk on aerial combat tactics.

The pilots of *Escadrille Américaine* learned a great deal from Nungesser and the other French pilots, and a few days after their arrival Bert Hall scored the squadron's second air victory. Hardly had his fellow pilots finished celebrating it than Bill Thaw racked up victory number three. He engaged a German Fokker pursuit plane in an air duel that began far behind the German lines, but ended up behind the French lines. By his dogged and skillful maneuvering, Thaw forced the Fokker pilot to continually "give air" toward the French lines in frantic efforts to avoid Thaw's deadly fire, which eventually sent him hurtling to earth in flames.

Shortly after Bill Thaw's victory five more American volunteer pilots joined *Escadrille Américaine* N. 124. They were Charles C. Johnson, of St. Louis, Missouri; Clyde Balsley, of San Antonio, Texas; Dudley Hill, of Peekskill, New York; Lawrence Rumsey, of Buffalo, New York; and Raoul Lufbery, of Wallingford, Connecticut, who was destined to become the most famous of all the Lafayette pilots.

Chapter
FIVE

Raoul Lufbery had one of the most colorful personalities of all the pilots who fought in the air in World War I. His adventurous, sometimes rebellious spirit had taken him to the four corners of the earth while he was still a very young man. Later this same spirit contributed to his being ranked as America's ace of aces, before his tragic death in May, 1918.

Lufbery was the only member of the Lafayette Flying Corps who was not an American by birth. He was born in France of French parents, but when he was very young his father moved to Wallingford, Connecticut, and became a naturalized American citizen. When Lufbery was only seventeen he rebelled against small-town life and ran away from home to see the world.

He first went to France and spent the next three years wandering about the land of his ancestors, paying his way by working at any odd job he could get. After he tired of France, Lufbery sailed from Marseilles to Algiers where he visited and worked for a while before traveling on to Tunis and Egypt, and then up through the Balkans to Germany. Eventually he went to South America where a letter from his father, telling of his mother's death, caught up with him. Wanting to see his father again, Lufbery returned to Wallingford, only to find that his father had set off on a world tour of his own. Raoul worked at odd jobs in Wallingford while waiting for his father to come home, but after a year had passed and his father had still not returned, Lufbery set out to roam some more himself.

This time he went to New Orleans, and on the spur of the moment enlisted in the regular army of the United States. He was sent to the Philippines, and while serving a two-year hitch he acquired a marksmanship skill which was to pay off years later in the skies over France. Lufbery became the best shot in his regiment and won every rifle shooting contest held by the U.S. armed forces stationed in the Philippines.

When his army enlistment was up, Lufbery traveled to Japan and then to China where he worked for the Chinese Customs Service. After a while, though, the desire to travel and see more new things took him to India where he got a job as a ticket agent in the Bombay railroad station. He soon lost that job, though, as the result of an action typical of his rebellious nature.

One day a pompous man in Indian dress came up to Lufbery's ticket window and just stood there staring hard at him.

"Do you want to buy a ticket?" Lufbery asked when the man didn't speak.

The Indian's eyes blazed and his lips thinned in anger. "When you speak to me, say *sir!*" he barked.

Reddening with anger, Lufbery strode out of his ticket booth. He grabbed the haughty Indian by the scruff of the neck and threw him out of the station. A few minutes later his boss called him into the office and fired him on the spot. The pompous man he had heaved out of the station happened to be the richest and most powerful merchant in the city of Bombay!

However, being out of a job was nothing new for Raoul

Lufbery. In a very short time he found another one in a department store. A month later, restless once more, he moved on to Calcutta. It was there he saw his first airplane—an experience which was to change the course of his life and give him for the first time a sense of purpose and direction.

The year was 1910 and the airplane was a Blériot monoplane owned by Marc Pourpe, a famous French stunt pilot. Pourpe had brought the Blériot out to Calcutta for an exhibition flight tour, but shortly after his arrival he'd met with double misfortune. First, his flying partner had been killed in a street accident in the city. Then, two days before Lufbery walked by the field and saw the parked airplane, Pourpe's mechanic had become so ill he had been forced to return at once to France.

When Lufbery joined a group of curious natives near the Blériot, he learned of Pourpe's plight. The French airman needed a mechanic immediately, or else he would have to cancel his tour. On learning that, the world-roaming American promptly walked up to Pourpe and offered his services. At first the Frenchman was delighted, but his attitude changed when, under questioning, Lufbery had to admit he didn't know a thing about airplane engines.

"Is this supposed to be a joke?" Pourpe said heatedly, starting to turn away.

"Just a minute!" Lufbery cried. "When you saw your first airplane did you know all about its engine? You had to learn, too, didn't you? Well, I can learn just as you did. I promise you, if you hire me as your mechanic you won't regret it!"

Raoul Lufbery's frank words both startled and impressed Pourpe. He scowled at the brash young man for a few moments, then decided to take a chance and hire him as his mechanic. Thus began a close association that was to last for four years.

During those years Pourpe and Lufbery toured all over

India and China with the Blériot monoplane. From the Orient the two went to Egypt where Pourpe piloted a history-making nonstop flight from Cairo to Khartoum, while Lufbery followed him on the ground via Nile steamer, cargo boat, camel, donkey, and train! Eventually, though, Pourpe's Blériot began to wear out and was no longer safe to take into the air. In the spring of 1914, Pourpe sold it for junk and took Lufbery to France with him to buy a new airplane which they planned to use on another long exhibition flight tour through the Orient.

That tour was never made. While Pourpe and Lufbery were in France awaiting the delivery of a Morane Parasol monoplane, the Germans smashed into Belgium and France declared war. Marc Pourpe immediately enlisted in the French Flying Service. That same day his new Morane Parasol was delivered to him and he was sent with it to the front to observe German troop movements through Luxembourg.

Lufbery tried to enlist in the French Flying Service so that he could serve as Pourpe's mechanic, but of course his American citizenship prevented it. He did the next best thing and enlisted in the French Foreign Legion, but he didn't see any front-line service with that hard-fighting group. Marc Pourpe was well known throughout France and had considerable influence with the high French military. As a result, seven days after Lufbery's Foreign Legion enlistment took effect he was transferred to the French Flying Service and dispatched to Marc Pourpe's front-line squadron to serve as his mechanic.

Lufbery served Pourpe as faithfully in war as he had in peace, until that day in December, 1914, when Marc Pourpe was shot down in flames behind the German lines. The death of his close friend was a terrible blow to Lufbery. It made him want to become a pilot himself so that he could carry on the fight Pourpe had given his life for. Lufbery went to his commanding officer and begged to be sent to flying school. His request was denied, however, because his services as an expert mechanic were so badly needed. But Lufbery wouldn't take no for an answer and he kept after his commanding officer, and any others he thought might help him, until finally his request was granted. On May 17, 1915, he was relieved of his mechanic's duties and sent to the French flying school at Chartres.

Because of the many things he had learned from Marc Pourpe during their long association, Lufbery progressed rapidly at the Chartres school. In two months' time he qualified on the Maurice Farman two-seater observation plane and was breveted pilot. Shortly after that he was sent to a French bombardment squadron stationed at the front. Although he did not shoot down any enemy planes while with the squadron, he soon proved himself to be one of its crack pilots. In fact, his flying skill attracted enough attention from his superiors so that he was chosen to go to the pursuit flying school at Le Plessis-Belleville to learn to fly the Nieuport single-seater.

He reported at Le Plessis-Belleville on April 10, 1916, and began his single-seater training. But to his surprise and chagrin, Lufbery experienced considerable difficulty in learning to fly the Nieuport pursuit plane. As a matter of fact, he was such a poor flight student that he came very close to being "washed out" and returned to his old bombardment squadron. In the end, though, by working hard and putting in extra hours he succeeded in learning to fly the tricky little Nieuport to the complete satisfaction of his instructors. And on May 24, 1916, he was sent to join *Escadrille Américaine* N. 124 at the Bar-le-Duc airfield on the Verdun front.

Lufbery's arrival at Bar-le-Duc, along with the four other American volunteer pilots, provided a big boost to the morale of the squadron's seven original pilots. The Germans on the other side of the front had increased the number of their air squadrons and were gaining a superiority in the air—at least in numbers. The flying skill and courage of the American pilots enabled them to continue to hold their own, but it was inevitable that sooner or later they would meet with casualties.

———

Bill Thaw was the first to be wounded in air battle. On the afternoon of the day he scored his first victory, and the third for the squadron, he again went on solo patrol, seeking still more action. When he was well past the German lines he sighted three German Fokker pursuits flying tight formation up and down their section of the front. Before taking off, Thaw had thought up a plan of his own for attacking an enemy plane, and he was eager to try it out. However, since there were three Fokkers below him, not just one, he would have to make some adjustments in his scheme. While he was busy figuring them out, the three Fokker pilots continued to fly up and down the front apparently oblivious to the lone Nieuport high above them.

Thaw settled on a new approach and climbed up even higher, maneuvering to get the sun behind him. Then he dropped the Nieuport's nose and went tearing down on the Fokkers, firing his gun without letup. Because the Germans could not see him coming down alone out of the sun, Thaw hoped they would think that several planes were diving on them. That was sure to confuse and alarm them, and when they frantically scattered for safety he would pick them off one by one.

The plan of attack worked . . . for a few seconds. The Fokker pilots were alarmed and they did break formation and start to scatter for safe air. But almost immediately they must have realized that only one plane was trying to drive them into the ground with wild gunfire. Each German pulled out of his dive for safety and went corkscrewing up in a climbing turn. The next thing Bill Thaw knew bullets were poking holes in his wings and slicing slivers off his struts from three different directions.

58

He flew the Nieuport as he had never flown it before in a desperate effort to break away from the bullet-spitting Fokkers and reach the safety of the French lines. For several horrible moments it looked as if he wasn't going to make it. Two of the Germans caught him in a savage cross fire and a bullet tore into his left arm. In one last frantic effort to get clear, Thaw flung the Nieuport into a steep power dive that threatened to tear the wings off. But fortunately the wings held on and he was able to outdive the Fokkers. Scooting at treetop level across the first and second lines of French trenches, he landed safely in front of the third line.

Exhausted by the three-to-one fight and suffering from the pain in his left arm, Thaw didn't even try to move for quite some time. The French soldiers in the third line of trenches, seeing him slumped motionless in the cockpit, thought he was dead and made no move to help him. Eventually, though, after he had finally made a few feeble attempts to hoist himself out of the plane, some of the soldiers rushed out of their trenches to his aid.

By the time they reached Thaw, German artillery was trying to zero in on the Nieuport and destroy it. With shells bursting all around, the French soldiers lifted Thaw out of the cockpit. He was close to fainting from loss of blood, and they had to carry him back to the first-aid dressing station. There his wound was given emergency treatment and he was put in an ambulance and driven to a Paris hospital. Luckily the wound proved not to be serious, and after only a few days in the hospital Thaw insisted upon being returned to his squadron at the front.

The second member of the American group to be wounded was Victor Chapman, in an air battle which took place shortly after Bill Thaw received his wound. Chapman was one of the most daring of the Lafayette pilots, and he often went out on patrol alone seeking action with the Germans regardless of

the odds against him. On this particular patrol he sighted five enemy planes a couple of thousand feet below him heading for the French side of the lines. Three German pursuit planes were escorting two observation planes.

No sooner did Chapman sight them than he went into action. Singling out one of the observation planes, he dived on it with his engine full out and the Lewis machine gun blazing. After the first burst of bullets the observation plane's pilot sent his aircraft scooting under the cover of the three escorting Fokkers. That maneuver didn't stop Chapman, however. He boldly tore down through the escorting Fokkers and hammered bullets into the two-seater until it fell to earth in flames.

Recovering quickly from their surprise, the three Fokker pilots thundered down on Chapman, who was now below them. They closed in on him from three different angles, and in a matter of moments his Nieuport was in danger of being shot out from under him. As Bill Thaw had done, Chapman hurled his plane first in one direction, then another, in a frantic effort to break away from the Fokkers. The relentless German fire filled his wings and fuselage full of holes, and made a shambles of his instrument panel.

Then a bullet struck and split in two a rod in the cockpit which connected with the plane's ailerons. Half of the rod ricocheted, slicing through Chapman's helmet and ripping a long gash in his scalp. With hardly any aileron control left, the Nieuport started into a spin toward the ground. Even though blood from his wound was half blinding Chapman, he managed to get hold of the two broken parts of the aileron control rod and hold them together with one hand. With his other hand he worked the joystick to get the Nieuport out of its spin. He started slip-sliding earthward to make it look as if the plane had been shot out of control and was going to crash.

The ruse fooled the German pilots. Certain that the Nieuport was finished, they started climbing back up to escort the remaining two-seater observation plane back home. Too late they saw Chapman recover from his trick maneuver and go gliding across No Man's Land to make a bumpy landing in a field behind the French lines.

Luckily he landed near a first-aid dressing station where his head wound was given emergency treatment. He was also fortunate enough to find someone nearby who could repair the broken aileron control rod. That afternoon, with his head covered by bandages, Chapman took off from the field in his shot-up Nieuport and flew safely back to the Bar-le-Duc airfield.

How the Nieuport managed to keep from falling apart on that return flight was one of the war's small miracles. When the squadron's mechanics examined it, they declared the bullet-riddled plane a total "washout" and almost not worth salvaging for spare parts. A new airplane would have to be obtained for Chapman. Since that would take a few days, his flying mates urged him to spend them in Paris on leave resting up. Chapman refused, insisting that his wound wasn't bothering him a bit. Besides, he said, there were plenty of things he could do on the ground while he waited for his new plane to arrive.

All things come in threes, it is said, and just two days after Victor Chapman's dogfight the third American pilot was wounded. He was Clyde Balsley, of San Antonio, Texas, who was often kidded by his flying mates because he personified the stereotype image of the dashing and debonair airman. Balsley was tall, handsome, perfectly groomed, and always wore a smart military mustache. In full uniform he reminded those meeting him for the first time of a spit-and-polish British army officer about to make an inspection of his troops.

In the middle of 1915 Balsley left his Texas home to go to France where he enlisted as an ambulance driver in the American Field Service. For four months he drove badly wounded

French soldiers from the front lines to the emergency first-aid station, most of the time under heavy German shellfire. At the end of those four months Balsley decided he could help France more by fighting than by driving an ambulance. Flying appealed to him, and he had heard rumors that a French squadron composed of American-born pilots was about to be formed. So on September 16, 1915, he resigned from the American Field Service and enlisted in the French Flying Service.

Like several other Americans before him, Balsley took his flight training at the Pau school. After four months he was breveted pilot on the Blériot monoplane and assigned to one of the squadrons of the Air Guard of Paris. He served with that squadron until May 29, 1916, when he joined *Escadrille Américaine* on the Verdun front. Three weeks later he made his first and last patrol over the German lines.

On that day, June 18, 1916, Captain Thénault, Norman Prince, Kiffin Rockwell, and Clyde Balsley took off together on an escort patrol. Several observation planes had been assigned to report the results of a French artillery bombardment, and it was the Nieuport pilots' job to protect them from attack by German aircraft. The mission was successfully accomplished without any German planes being sighted. But when Captain Thénault and his American pilots were heading for home at some eleven thousand feet they met a large formation of German two-seater and pursuit planes. In no time at all the air battle was on.

According to Balsley's own story of the air fight, he suddenly found himself just above and behind a German Aviatik observation plane. He dived on the enemy plane, and since neither the German pilot nor the observer seemed aware of him, it looked like an easy victory. When he was less than a hundred feet from the Aviatik he opened fire—but only a single bullet ripped out of his Lewis machine gun before it jammed!

Pulling out of his dive and off to one side, Balsley tried frantically to clear the jammed gun and make a second attack while there was still time. But the German pilot had become aware of him, guessed that his gun was jammed, and zoomed up after him with his own gun blazing. Another German pilot had also spotted him and was cutting in on him from the side, raking the plane with his machine gun. For a few precious moments Balsley managed to evade the fire of the two Germans while he continued to try to clear his jammed gun. But suddenly he was struck in the left hip by an explosive bullet. It made a terrible wound, shattering the sciatic nerve and sending fiery pain shooting through his entire body.

Almost fainting from the pain, and with his left leg completely paralyzed, Balsley tried to work the rudder of his Nieuport by grasping the useless left leg with his two hands and pushing it against the rudder bar. Fortunately for him the attention of his attackers had been diverted elsewhere; otherwise he would almost certainly have been shot out of the air. As it was, he found himself alone and still some six thousand feet above what he believed to be the French lines. Flying the Nieuport as best he could, he brought it down and attempted to make a landing behind the second line of trenches. He almost made it, but at the last moment the Nieuport struck an obstacle on the ground and went flipping over on its back. The almost unconscious Balsley was thrown out of the cockpit.

As he lay crumpled on the shell-pocked ground, he was suddenly not at all sure he had crash-landed on French ground. Gritting his teeth against the excruciating pain, he slowly dragged himself down into an old shell hole. Moments later he knew for certain he was on French ground when German artillery shells started dropping down in search of the Nieuport. Unable to move out of the shell hole because of the pain and the German fire, Balsley lay there helpless for over an hour.

Then some brave French soldiers crawled from their trench to rescue him.

They carried him back to the emergency first-aid station where his terrible wound was treated as well as it could be under the circumstances. Later he was put in an ambulance and driven to the French military hospital at Vadelaincourt where his life hung in the balance for several days. He slowly recovered, but during the next twelve months he was operated on six times for the removal of explosive bullet splinters embedded deep in his body.

In late 1917, almost eighteen months after his first and last air battle, Balsley had recovered sufficiently to be returned to his home in Texas. He took with him as a grim souvenir eleven bits of explosive bullet metal which had been removed from his body by the French doctors.

Clyde Balsley was the first member of *Escadrille Américaine* to be seriously wounded in the air war. He was also the first American known to be hit by an explosive bullet, which, incidentally, had been outlawed by the Geneva Convention as a weapon of war long before the start of World War I.

While Balsley was in the Vadelaincourt military hospital fighting for his life, he also unknowingly played a part in a series of events which resulted in death striking the pilots of *Escadrille Américaine* for the first time.

Chapter
SIX

The first member of the Lafayette Flying Corps to die in aerial combat was Victor Chapman, one of the original seven pilots of *Escadrille Américaine*. His comrades often called Chapman "the fightingest guy in the war"—a reputation justified by such actions as his daring solo dogfight with five German planes which was recounted in the previous chapter.

Perhaps Chapman's bravery and sense of purpose were qualities handed down to him by his forebears. His great-great-grandfather was John Jay, one of the signers of the Declaration of Independence, a member of the Continental Congress, and a close friend of Benjamin Franklin. His father was John Jay Chapman, a famed essayist and poet, who was regarded in his time as one of the finest American writers.

As a youth Chapman traveled extensively in Europe with his parents, and after his graduation from Harvard he went to France to study architecture at the École des Beaux-Arts in Paris. In the summer of 1914 he joined his parents in England for a vacation tour, but before it was completed World War I broke out. Upon hearing the news Chapman returned immediately to France and enlisted in the French Foreign Legion.

He served with the Legion for a year, spending most of that time in sectors where the fighting was hottest. Even at the beginning of his war career, the complete defeat of the enemy was almost an obsession with Chapman, and he refused to spare himself in any way. His dedication as a soldier is revealed in the story of an event which occurred during his Foreign Legion service, when he was a member of a patrol that worked its way deep behind the German lines to obtain valuable information.

Before the patrol reached its objective it was spotted by the Germans and fired upon. A machine gun bullet went through the muscles of Chapman's lower right arm. One of his comrades gave him first aid and urged him to start crawling back toward the French lines. Chapman ignored his friend's advice and completed the patrol, returning only when the others did and without saying a thing about his wound. Later when one of his officers saw that he was wounded, Chapman refused to be sent to the rear for hospital treatment and insisted on remaining with his company in the front lines.

During his service with the Foreign Legion Chapman became expert with both the rifle and the machine gun. Day after day he gave a good account of himself in battle, but he found himself growing more and more fascinated by the airplanes twisting and turning in the sky above the trenches. Like other Americans before him, he began to long for an opportunity to fight for France in the air.

When he heard about Norman Prince's plan to form an all-American squadron, Chapman immediately put in a request for his release from the French Foreign Legion and a transfer to the French Flying Service. It was granted on August 1, 1915.

As his first assignment in the Flying Service, Chapman expected that he would be given flight instruction—but disappointment awaited him. Because of his remarkable ability with a machine gun he was removed from the roster of student pilots and sent straight to a French Voisin bomber squadron at the front to serve as an aerial machine gunner. During the next month Chapman flew several long-distance flights with the squadron and capably performed all his aerial machine gunner duties. At the end of that time, though, his repeated request for transfer was granted and he was sent to the flying school at Avord for flight training. On January 9, 1916, he was breveted a pilot on the French Maurice Farman biplane, and on April 20, together with the six other American pioneers of *Escadrille Américaine* N. 124, he reported for duty at the Luxeuil front.

Victor Chapman's career as a pursuit pilot lasted only two months and three days, but during that time he flew more patrols against the Germans than any other member of the squadron. He was in the air almost constantly, either escorting bombers and observation planes, or patrolling alone deep in German-held air. The first off the ground and the last to come home, he usually returned with only a few drops of fuel left in his tank. The Nieuport's tank carried enough fuel for two hours of flight, and it was not unusual for Chapman to make four and five patrols a day. As long as there was any daylight left he would be in the air hunting for Germans.

Chapman received official credit for only one German plane shot down. That was the Fokker he destroyed on June 17, 1916, when he boldly attacked five German aircraft. However, he participated in countless other air battles far behind the German lines and, as in the case of other Lafayette pilots, he undoubtedly scored several unconfirmed victories.

Although he might well have vaunted his courage and daring, Chapman was extremely modest and shy and never did anything to deliberately attract attention. He was decorated for deeds of valor while serving with the Foreign Legion, and also for his later exploits in the air, but he very seldom wore his medal ribbons and never talked about receiving any awards. Of all Victor Chapman's attributes, however, perhaps the finest were his thoughtfulness for those who flew and fought with him, and his readiness to help out a friend at any time.

Ironically enough it was these very qualities that indirectly led to Chapman's death in the air.

Two days after Clyde Balsley was taken to the military hospital at Vadelaincourt, suffering from the German explosive bullet wound in his hip, Victor Chapman flew over to visit him. Before going to see his friend, Chapman talked with the doctors and on learning the seriousness of Balsley's condition, he realized that any show of sympathy would only make his squadron mate feel worse. Instead, he adopted a pose of good-natured envy as he entered the hospital ward.

"Well, look who's taking a little rest from the war!" he exclaimed when he reached the bedside of the half-dozing Balsley.

The hearty, familiar voice roused Balsley. "Hey, am I glad to see you, Victor!" he said.

"I've brought you some of your toilet articles." Chapman handed the injured man a neatly wrapped parcel. "If there's anything else you want, just name it and I'll bring it over next trip."

"I guess there's nothing I really need," Balsley whispered, "except—I get so thirsty. They won't let me drink anything— all I can do is suck on a wet cloth."

Chapman gently pressed his friend's shoulder. "Easy does it, Clyde," he said soothingly. "Just try and relax, fellow. Everything's going to be fine. The doctors are working wonders with you and you'll be out of here in no time. Tell you what—I'll pop over here tomorrow with some oranges for you to suck on. I'm sure that will be okay with the doctors, and it should help cure your thirst."

"*Oranges?*" Balsley gasped. "Are you kidding? Where in

the world are you going to get any oranges, Vic?"

Chapman winked. "Just leave that to me," he replied. "I'll get hold of some, and that's a promise. Now you just relax and get some more sleep. I'll see you again tomorrow—with oranges!"

Clyde Balsley smiled in anticipation but he didn't say anything. The visit by Chapman, short as it was, had taxed his strength. He closed his eyes once more, and Chapman walked silently out of the ward.

The following morning Balsley had three other visitors— Captain Thénault, accompanied by a French army colonel and a major. Balsley's first thought was that Victor Chapman had been unable to come with the oranges himself and had sent them over by the squadron's commander. But why a strange French army colonel and major had come along he had no idea.

"We have a present for you," Captain Thénault said, smiling down at him.

Balsley returned the smile and nodded weakly. "Yes, I know," he said. "Good old Victor!"

Captain Thénault gave him a slightly puzzled look, but he didn't say anything. Instead he stepped back from the bed and let the French army colonel take his place. The colonel made a short speech and then proceeded to decorate Balsley with the *Médaille Militaire* and the *Croix de Guerre*. As the colonel stepped back and solemnly saluted him Balsley stared down at the medals pinned to his hospital gown. A mixture of dumbfounded astonishment and cold fear surged through him, and it was a moment or two before he could find his tongue.

"What . . . what are they for?" he finally gasped. "I haven't done anything."

"Oh, but you have," the colonel quickly interjected. "You have fought with honor for France, a country not your own. You have destroyed an enemy of France, and you have shed your blood in battle."

70

The colonel had some more complimentary things to say, but Clyde Balsley barely listened to them. A hundred and one thoughts were racing through his head, all of them more than a little disturbing. He had not shot down any enemy airplane, so why had the colonel said he had . . . and decorated him with the two medals? Only yesterday two wounded French soldiers had been decorated . . . *shortly before they died.* Had the hospital doctors been keeping the truth from him? Was he so severely wounded that he was going to die? Was this little ceremony actually a good-by tribute?

As the disturbing thoughts churned through his head Balsley suddenly realized the French officers were staring down at him expectantly, and waiting. He swallowed and licked his lips. "Thank you," he said with an effort. Then he blurted out, "But I am not going to die!"

His burst of words startled the three French officers, but they quickly regained their composure. Sensing how upset Balsley was, they reassured him that he most certainly was not going to die, and would very soon be flying again for France. Eventually they took their leave and left Balsley with his medals.

Meantime Victor Chapman had not forgotten his promise to get hold of some oranges for Balsley. How Chapman managed to obtain a whole basket of the fruit is not recorded, but it is believed he drove a squadron car all the way to Paris in the early hours of the morning and bought them there. At any rate, by breakfast time Chapman had a basket of oranges, but he was unable to fly them over to Balsley's hospital right away.

There was considerable air activity over the front and Chapman made several patrols across the lines. By noon, though, the air fighting had died down, and after lunch he made ready to fly the oranges over to Balsley. As he was stowing the basket behind his seat he suddenly noticed that Captain Thénault, Norman Prince, and Raoul Lufbery were about to take off on another patrol. Jumping down from the fuselage step of his

Nieuport, he ran over to the nearest plane, which happened to be Captain Thénault's.

"Wait for me and I'll go with you!" he called up to the squadron commander, who was seated in the cockpit. "I'm on my way to Balsley with some oranges, but first I'll go along with you, in case you run into something. If there's nothing stirring, then I'll break away and head for the hospital."

Captain Thénault shook his head, smiling. "No, don't bother to do that, Victor," he said. "You've already made enough patrols for one day. You go on and take your oranges over to Balsley."

Captain Thénault waved his hand in signal to Prince and Lufbery, and the three of them took off. Since the mechanics had not finished readying his Nieuport for flight, Chapman stood where he was for a few moments watching the other three planes climb for altitude on their way to the front. When they were lost to view in the high air, he went to his own plane to start the engine and get it warmed up for take-off. Then he took the fleet little Nieuport up into the air—but instead of heading in the direction of Clyde Balsley's hospital he flew in pursuit of his three squadron mates.

By the time Chapman took off, Captain Thénault, Prince, and Lufbery had reached the German lines. They flew on deep into German-held air and presently sighted two German observation planes headed for the French lines. Unfortunately, though, they failed to spot a flight of six German Fokkers hiding in the high sun, and when they went diving down on the observation planes, the Fokkers came wing screaming down on them!

In a matter of seconds the air was filled with aircraft twisting and turning about. Caught by surprise by the attacking Fokkers, Captain Thénault and his two American pilots had to call upon all their flying skills to escape the hail of enemy bullets. They succeeded in shooting and flying their way out of

the German trap, and as soon as they had shaken off the Fokkers, Captain Thénault wisely decided against engaging in another battle. The odds were two to one against them, and they were running low on fuel, besides. They had succeeded in driving the German observation planes away from the French lines and that, after all, was their main task. So the French commander of the American Squadron signaled his two pilots to form a tight formation, and led the way back to their home airfield.

Victor Chapman wasn't at the field when they landed, and he didn't put in an appearance during the afternoon hours, either. When darkness began to settle down he still had not returned from what his flying mates thought had been a trip to Clyde Balsley's hospital.

The pilots of *Escadrille Américaine* weren't alarmed, however. It was nothing unusual for Chapman's Nieuport to be the last plane to land at the end of a day's flying. More than once the squadron's mechanics had had to set out oil pot flares to indicate the wind direction and give him enough light to land by. Everyone simply assumed that Chapman had had an extra long visit with Balsley at the hospital, and would be buzzing the field soon in signal for the mechanics to set out the flares.

But two hours passed and still no airplane had buzzed the field when a phone call came for Captain Thénault. It was the commanding officer of a French Farman observation plane squadron, calling to inform a stunned Captain Thénault that Victor Chapman was dead. He had died that afternoon when he singlehandedly attacked six diving German Fokkers. His plane went hurtling on down to earth, where it crashed and burst into flames.

Just before the tragedy occurred, the pilot of one of the French observation planes had seen three Nieuports with *Escadrille Américaine* insignia make a formation attack on two

German observation planes headed for the French lines. Seconds later he saw six German Fokkers drop out of the sun and go diving down on the Nieuports. At almost the same instant, though, a fourth *Escadrille Américaine* Nieuport that had been flying even higher dived straight down on the attacking Fokkers. Exactly what happened the French observation plane pilot was unable to say, but the pilot of the single Nieuport never pulled out of his dive. And obviously his fellow American pilots had failed to see him.

Apparently Victor Chapman had reached the area of the sky where the six German Fokkers were poised for their attack down out of the sun on Captain Thénault, Prince, and Lufbery. Realizing instantly that his squadron mates were unaware of the diving enemy planes, Chapman had hurled his Nieuport at the Germans in a desperate effort to protect his comrades.

Why he lost control of his plane and crashed will never be known. He may have been killed instantly by the fire of one of the diving Fokkers, or perhaps something went wrong with his plane or its engine. But whatever the explanation, one thing is absolutely certain. Victor Chapman sacrificed his own life in a gallant attempt to protect the lives of his flying mates. And it is quite possible that his brave singlehanded attack on the six diving Fokkers was responsible for spoiling their aim and enabling Captain Thénault, Norman Prince, and Raoul Lufbery to get safely away.

Victor Chapman's death was a terrible blow to every member of *Escadrille Américaine*. He had been loved by officers, noncoms, and enlisted men alike. It was planned that if and when the French forces captured the area where he had crashed, Chapman's grave would be found and he would be given a second and full military funeral by his squadron. That never happened, however. Some weeks later the French ground forces did capture the area where he had fallen, but his grave was never located, nor any German record of his burial. Chapman was the first of seven Lafayette Flying Corps pilots who were shot down by the Germans and whose remains were never found.

Of the twelve American pilots who made up the flying roster of *Escadrille Américaine,* only nine were now on active duty. Victor Chapman was dead, Clyde Balsley was in the hospital, and so was Jim McConnell, who had wrenched his back badly in a crash landing. However, the nine remaining pilots, far from lessening their efforts, kept adding to the squadron's already impressive record. In the next few months Bert Hall and Norman Prince won their second and third air victories, and Kiffin Rockwell got his second. And it was shortly after Victor Chapman's tragic death that Raoul Lufbery began to rack up his string of amazing air victories. By October when the squadron was relieved of duty at the Bar-le-Duc field and sent to its old field at Luxeuil, where German air activity had suddenly increased, Lufbery had shot down five officially confirmed enemy planes, to become the first American air ace in World War I.

Before the pilots of *Escadrille Américaine* reported to Luxeuil they spent a few days of well-earned leave in Paris. As usual the men enjoyed a relaxing break in their routine, but this time a little something new was added. The pilots acquired a squadron mascot—a four-month-old male lion cub, which they named Whiskey.

The story goes that Whiskey was born on a boat carrying animals from Africa to France for subsequent sale to French zoos. Because of the war, there wasn't much demand for the animals and they were advertised for sale in French newspapers. Two of the *Escadrille Américaine* pilots saw the ad in a Paris newspaper and decided that the young lion cub which was described would make a great mascot for the squadron. The squadron already had a number of pets, including dogs, cats, birds, parrots, and even a goat. A real live lion cub, though, would be something unique, and the two men who had read the ad lost no time in convincing the others that it was a good idea. Everybody dug down deep and the combined effort netted the five hundred francs needed to buy Whiskey.

During the remainder of their leave the pilots took Whiskey with them everywhere they went, and to say that he caused a stir would be putting it mildly. He was a cute and frisky little fellow who loved to have a fuss made over him, but when he wanted to he could let out a roar that would stiffen the hair of those seeing him for the first time. In no time at all Raoul Lufbery, to whom Whiskey had taken a special liking, taught the cub to roar on signal—a quick jerk on the leash. After that the fun-seeking American pilots would have Whiskey enter a restaurant or café first, get him to let out a lusty roar by jerking his leash, and watch the other customers make for the nearest exit.

On one occasion, though, Whiskey's roaring trick backfired. It happened when the pilots were boarding the train for Luxeuil at the end of their short Paris leave. They kept Whiskey hidden, planning to scare the conductor when he came along to collect tickets. But the joke didn't work as planned. Whiskey let out a very frightening roar on signal, but the conductor didn't even change expression. Without a word he scooped up the lion cub, leash and all, and took him back to the baggage car where he remained for the rest of the trip, with the rather chagrined American pilots taking turns feeding him and keeping him company!

Chapter
SEVEN

When the pilots of *Escadrille Américaine* arrived at Luxeuil, almost the entire town turned out to meet them at the station and welcome them back. For those who had been stationed there before, it was a little like Old Home Week. All traces of the damage caused by the German air raid the night before they left for Bar-le-Duc had disappeared and the over-all appearance of the airfield was just as they remembered it. There was, however, one new addition. A bombing group of the British Royal Naval Air Service, consisting of some fifty pilots and close to a thousand enlisted men, was now stationed at the Luxeuil field. It had been temporarily attached to the French Air Service for combined bombing raids over the German lines.

As all the British pilots were officers, while most of the American pilots were only corporals or sergeants, the British at first held themselves aloof. The friendliness of the Americans soon broke the ice, however, and in no time at all both groups were throwing get-together parties for each other. A close bond of friendship eventually developed between the two groups, and it increased day by day as they flew together against the Germans.

78

Several weeks passed, though, before the *Escadrille Américaine* pilots were able to do any flying. They had been ordered to leave their old Nieuport 17s at the Bar-le-Duc field, since the squadron was to be fitted out with the brand-new Nieuport 27s. The new type of Nieuport was supposed to be waiting for them when they arrived at Luxeuil, but due to some foul-up the new planes didn't begin to arrive until two weeks later. As soon as the pilots saw them, however, they all agreed that the new models were well worth waiting for.

The Nieuport 27 was a big improvement on the old Nieuport 17. It had a greater wing area, and was driven by a more powerful Le Rhône rotary engine that gave it an increase in speed of fifteen miles an hour. It could gain altitude much faster, climb to a service ceiling of eighteen thousand feet, and was much more maneuverable than the Nieuport 17.

Another improvement was the British Vickers aerial machine gun that was synchronized to shoot between the whirling blades of the propeller. The device was called the Constantinesco synchronized gear and was first used by the British Royal Flying Corps. It consisted of a cam, or rotating piece, fitted to the propeller shaft; an oil-filled tube with a plunger at both ends that led from the cam to the machine gun trigger; and a cylinder of oil under constant plunger spring pressure that was released into the tube line when the pilot pressed the firing lever attached to his joystick.

Whenever the firing lever was pressed, the oil in the tube line was put under instant pressure. Then each time the cam on the propeller shaft struck the plunger, a pulsation was sent to the plunger's other end which tripped the machine gun's trigger and fired it. Releasing the firing lever of course cut off pressure in the tube and the machine gun stopped firing. The cam was fitted to the propeller shaft at a point where the trailing edge of the blade was directly in front of the line of fire.

By the time the cam had sent a pulsation of oil to the machine gun's trigger, the blade had just passed the line of fire and the bullet went safely between the whirling blades.

As soon as the new Nieuport 27s arrived, the American pilots worked day and night with their mechanics to get them in shape for war patrol and combat work. Raoul Lufbery and Kiffin Rockwell were the first to finish, and on September 23 they took off together on the squadron's first patrol since returning to the Luxeuil airfield. Unfortunately, that day was to be one of the saddest of the entire war for the pilots of *Escadrille Américaine*.

Because of dense clouds Lufbery and Rockwell became separated as they were crossing the German lines, and they never saw each other again. Each continued his patrol alone, and Kiffin Rockwell's effort was destined to be his last. What happened to him was later reported by a French artillery officer who saw it all through field glasses.

According to the French officer, Rockwell came upon a lumbering German observation plane a few thousand feet below him just after he'd crossed over the enemy lines. He did not immediately attack, but circled about for a few moments instead. Rockwell was cautious because the Germans had lately adopted the trick of sending out a slow-moving two-seater observation plane as bait to lure down some unsuspecting Allied pilot. Then German fighter pilots hiding upstairs in the sun could pounce on him and finish him off.

On this occasion, though, the German two-seater observation plane was not serving as trap bait. When Rockwell finally dropped his nose and dived on it, no Germans up in the sun came piling down to attack him. But the pilot of the German two-seater became aware of Rockwell diving on him and tried to break away while his observer fired the rear gun at the diving Nieuport. Rockwell stuck right with him, but withheld his fire

80

until it looked as if he would dive straight into the German airplane. At the last moment, though, he started shooting and the French artillery officer who was watching the engagement saw the German plane stagger in the air and fall over on one wing as though about to go spinning down to the ground.

The German two-seater did not fall into a spin, however. The pilot pulled it up onto even keel and headed east toward his home field as fast as he could go. To the French artillery officer it looked as if Rockwell was starting another diving attack on the fleeing German plane when something happened. His Nieuport suddenly nosed down in an almost vertical dive toward the ground. Seconds later the wings on the right side broke off and went fluttering down through the air. With the wings gone, Kiffin Rockwell was doomed. His crippled Nieuport dropped like a rock and crashed in a field of flowers three hundred yards inside the French lines.

As so often happened, shortly after Rockwell's plane smashed into the ground German guns opened fire on the spot just in case the pilot was still alive, or the plane not damaged enough to make it a total loss. Despite the shells exploding around them, French soldiers ran to Rockwell's crashed plane, lifted the dead American out and carried him away from the firing area. The French doctor who examined Rockwell's body found a deep wound in his chest which he said had been caused by a German explosive bullet. An ordinary bullet would have wounded Rockwell badly, too, but would probably not have prevented him from keeping control of his plane and making a safe landing on the French side of the lines. The outlawed explosive bullet killed him instantly, though, and his dead body must have slumped forward against the joystick. That sent the Nieuport into a vertical dive which soon proved too great a strain for the small plane to stand, and as a result the right wings tore off.

After Raoul Lufbery and Kiffin Rockwell had become separated in the clouds, Lufbery circled about for some minutes trying to find his companion. When he failed to do so, he flew on deep into German air and presently sighted a lone enemy plane. Before he could get close enough to open fire on it, two German Fokkers jumped him and he had to do some fancy dogfight flying just to hold his own against the pair. But hold his own he did until all his ammunition was gone and the fuel in his tank was dangerously low. Only then did he break away from the two circling Fokker pilots and high-tail it for the safety of the French lines. Lufbery just barely made it. As he crossed over the French trenches his engine quit cold from lack of gas, but since he still had considerable altitude he was able to glide well behind the lines and land safely in a field near the town of Fontaine.

Learning that it would be some time before he would be able to obtain gas for his plane, Lufbery called the Luxeuil airfield to let them know what had happened and where he was. Word of Kiffin Rockwell's death had already reached Luxeuil, and when Lufbery was told of it over the phone he was shocked and angry.

A French airfield was near Fontaine, and Lufbery hitchhiked there to plead with the commanding officer for gas and ammunition for his Nieuport. At first the commanding officer refused the wild-eyed American pilot, but eventually he gave in. Within an hour the Nieuport was refueled and rearmed, and Raoul Lufbery was back in the air again heading for the German lines. When he reached them he crossed over and started flying up and down the front in search of enemy planes. Finding none, he flew deeper and deeper into German-held air, but still didn't sight any German planes. He even sought out a German airfield far behind the front and dived on it in challenge for any German to come up and give battle. No German pilots accepted the challenge, however, and finally, with gas running low again, Lufbery was forced to give up his hunt for revenge and fly back to the Luxeuil airfield.

The death in the air of Kiffin Rockwell hit the pilots of *Escadrille Américaine* every bit as hard as had the death of Victor Chapman. Like Chapman, Rockwell inspired others with his comradeship, courage, and complete dedication to the cause for which they were all fighting. One of the finest tributes paid to any World War I pilot was the comment of a squadron mate who said of him, "When Kiffin Rockwell was in the air, no German passed."

Perhaps it was just a coincidence, but the night before Kiffin Rockwell died he made the statement that if he were ever shot down he would like to be buried where his plane crashed. His fellow pilots wanted to grant his desire, but it was impossible for them to do so. His plane had crashed much too close to the lines, and a funeral party would undoubtedly be shelled by enemy guns and good men needlessly killed. Instead, Rockwell's body, covered by an American flag, was returned to Luxeuil where he was given a full military funeral. The entire British Royal Naval Air Service unit stationed at the airfield marched in his honor, as did a whole battalion of French troops. The people of Luxeuil also walked behind the bier, and many pilots from nearby French Flying Service fields flew over the grave and dropped flowers in farewell tribute to a brave man who had come from a distant land to help them fight for their liberty.

When the pilots of *Escadrille Américaine* took to the air again after Rockwell's funeral, they were all determined to avenge the death of their flying comrade. Norman Prince scored first, and because of its unusualness, his victory was long remembered by his fellow pilots.

Prince made this particular patrol on the afternoon of the day of Rockwell's funeral. It was a solo patrol over the enemy lines, and hardly had Prince crossed them when he spotted a lone German observation plane flying serenely along as if its pilot and observer were completely oblivious to the war. Suspecting the usual baited trap, Prince took his time and made very sure there was no other German plane in the surrounding sky. Then he dropped the Nieuport's nose and went rocketing down on the cruising enemy two-seater.

His first burst of fire killed the German observer. With his tail unprotected, the German pilot started throwing his airplane about in a frantic effort to get clear of the Nieuport and its blazing Vickers machine gun. In a few seconds the German pilot must have realized he would never escape alive, because he suddenly quit cold and did an amazing thing. He leveled off his plane and then stood up in the cockpit with both hands raised high over his head in a signal of complete surrender.

At first Prince simply couldn't believe it. Then the meaning of the German's signal sank home. Holding his fire, but ready for anything, Prince flew in close to the German two-seater and motioned to its pilot to fly toward the French lines. The German instantly obeyed, and with Norman Prince riding his tail every foot of the way, he flew his two-seater across the French lines. On another signal from Prince, he landed it in a field where French soldiers took him prisoner and captured his airplane intact.

Later, when he was describing the strange affair to his fellow pilots, Prince frankly admitted that for a moment or two sorrow and anger over Kiffin Rockwell's death had almost caused him to shoot down the surrendering German in cold blood. But two things prevented him from doing it: his better nature, which told him it would be wrong; and the sudden realization that no one in *Escadrille Américaine* N. 124 had yet succeeded in forcing down a German plane intact behind the French lines. If he could get this German to land, the pilots of

the *Escadrille,* not to mention the French Flying Service technical experts, would be able to make a complete examination of the captured plane and gain a knowledge of its good and bad features which might be useful to them in future encounters with that type of enemy aircraft.

A few days after Kiffin Rockwell's funeral and Norman Prince's startling victory, Bert Hall downed another German plane. Hall was patrolling the French lines when he sighted a lone German two-seater Aviatik trying to sneak across to take some pictures. After making sure there were no enemy fighters waiting for him in the high sky, Hall attacked the Aviatik with gun blazing. In a matter of seconds the battle was over. The German two-seater became a ball of fire that fell to the ground well within view of French troops in the front line.

That was Hall's third officially confirmed victory and, as far as Lafayette Flying Corps records are concerned, the last he was to score in the war. It is possible, though, that he may have shot down other enemy planes in unobserved encounters. In November, 1916, Hall suddenly left *Escadrille Américaine,* for reasons which were not made public, to join a French squadron, and a year later he turned up mysteriously in the United States. After that he never returned to the war.

From the very beginning of his war career Bert Hall was, according to those who knew him, a puzzling character, a combination of rebel and man of mystery. In August, 1914, the very first month of the war, he enlisted in the French Foreign Legion, claiming that he had already seen military service in the Turkish-Bulgarian war in 1912. Whether or not that was true was never established, but French Foreign Legion records do show that he served with distinction in that hard-fighting unit.

Like Bill Thaw and Jimmy Bach, Bert Hall was soon attracted to the flying side of the war, and on December 28, 1914, he transferred from the Legion to the French Flying Service. He was breveted a pilot on August 19, 1915, and saw active service with two French Morane Parasol squadrons before he became one of the seven original members of *Escadrille Américaine* N. 124.

During the seven months Hall was with the American squadron he was a willing and daring pilot at all times. He downed three enemy planes officially, and probably as many or more unofficially. But his sudden leave-taking of *Escadrille Américaine* in November of 1916 was, and still is, clouded in mystery, as is the remainder of his war service. It was reported that in early 1917 he became a member of a French military aviation commission which went to Rumania. However, it was also reported at the time that he had gone to Russia instead. It is a known fact, though, that in late 1917 he received permission from the French Government to return to the United States to enlist in his own country's forces. But he never did enlist. His name does not appear on any of the rosters of the U.S. armed forces in World War I, nor is there any record of what happened to this fine combat pilot after he arrived back in his home country.

Bert Hall's third and last air victory was *Escadrille Américaine's* thirteenth since becoming a front-line squadron on April 20, 1916. And two days later Norman Prince got his second confirmed victory, to boost the total up to fourteen. It was a record all the pilots could be justly proud of, for it proved that the little group of American volunteers could fly wing to wing with the very best of France's air squadrons and more than hold their own against anything the Germans sent against them.

But fourteen official air victories was only the beginning. There were still twelve times that many to go, and much more furious air action than the squadron had experienced thus far.

The American pilots got a good sample of what lay ahead when *Escadrille Américaine* N. 124 was assigned to play a vital role in a long and carefully planned joint Allied air offensive against the German forces.

Chapter
EIGHT

The Allied air offensive began on October 12, 1916, with an eighty-plane bombing raid on the German Mauser Arms Works at Oberndorf. Most of the bombers were British Sopwith biplanes flown by Royal Naval Air Service pilots. The Sopwith biplane was ordinarily a two-seater, but on this particular raid they were flown solo so that four instead of three 100-pound bombs could be carried. The rest of the bombers were French Bréguets and Farmans, each capable of carrying a ton or more of bombs.

Several French pursuit squadrons were to serve as escorts for the bombers on the daring raid which would be made in broad daylight. Because of their limited fuel supply, the pursuit planes would escort the bombers as close to the target as they could, then return to emergency fields just behind the French lines to refuel. At a prearranged time they would take off again and fly out to meet the returning bombers and escort them the rest of the way home.

One of the French pursuit squadrons assigned to bomber escort work was *Escadrille Américaine*. Unfortunately, though, only four of the squadron's Nieuports were in flying condition.

They belonged to Lt. de Laage de Meux, the squadron's French adjutant, Norman Prince, Raoul Lufbery, and Didier Masson, who had joined the squadron in June.

Masson came from Los Angeles, California, and next to Raoul Lufbery, was one of the most colorful characters to wear the French uniform in World War I. The son of French-born parents, Masson set out to see the world on his own as soon as he was old enough to take care of himself. He went to France in 1909 to visit the land of his parents, and while there became interested in aviation. He learned to fly the Antoinette monoplane, and in 1911 when he returned to the United States he became engaged in exhibition flying in his native California.

By 1913, Didier Masson had tired of exhibition flying and he started looking around for more exciting things to do. Down in Mexico at that time Gen. Alvaro Obregon was trying to establish a stable government, while his sworn enemy, Gen. Victoriano Huerta, was exerting every effort to topple him from power. Hearing of their conflict, Masson went to Mexico to offer his flying services to General Obregon, the recognized leader of the country. He took along with him an English soldier-of-fortune named Tommy Dean who was a good airplane mechanic. He also brought with him an old Curtiss biplane which, so the story goes, was smuggled across the border in pieces and reassembled on Mexican soil.

For almost a year Masson and Dean and the battered Curtiss biplane served as General Obregon's entire air force. Their main job was to seek out General Huerta's guerrilla forces and attack them with homemade bombs. How much success Didier Masson had on his one-plane bombing raids was never officially recorded, but in early 1914 he quit General Obregon and started to fly for one Venustiano Carranza, who was waging a private war in the north with the famous Mexican bandit, Francisco (Pancho) Villa. Soon afterward, though, war clouds began to gather over Europe, and Didier quit his job with Carranza in order to sail for France.

Arriving there just as war broke out, Masson at once offered his services to the French Government. Strangely enough, he did not apply for enlistment in the French Flying Service. Instead he enlisted in the French infantry and, for reasons never explained, was accepted even though he was of American birth. He served with distinction in the 129th and 36th French Infantry Regiments until October of the first year of the war. At that time he obtained his transfer from the infantry to the French Air Service and was sent to the Pau flying school for training.

Because of his flying experience in California and Mexico, Didier expected to have a relatively easy time in flight school, but such was not the case. For some strange reason (again like Raoul Lufbery) he had difficulty handling the French aircraft, and not until May, 1915, was he breveted a pilot and assigned to a French Caudron squadron at the front. He flew the French bomber at the front until September, at which time he asked and was given permission to go to a pursuit flying school. When he graduated from the pursuit school, he returned to the front as a member of French Nieuport Squadron No. 68, and in June of 1916 he was transferred to *Escadrille Américaine* N. 124. Four months of flying with the *Escadrille* had made Masson a seasoned veteran by the time the squadron was assigned to its first major raid in October.

The Allied bombing of the German Mauser Arms Works at Oberndorf turned out to be a tremendous success. The fleets of British Sopwiths and French Bréguets and Farmans took off from different fields and joined forces in the air. Since the small Nieuport pursuit planes carried only a two-hour supply of fuel, they had to wait until the last minute before taking off to catch up with the bombers and escort them east to the Rhine River.

The German air squadrons guarding that section of the front were taken by complete surprise. Only a very few German planes were in the air, and the huge bombing armada and its escort were well on their way toward the target before the Germans realized what was happening. When they did, though, they sent aloft every plane they could muster in a desperate attempt to halt the Allied armada. A terrific air battle ensued, one that cost the Allies six bombing planes. The Germans also paid a heavy price, losing at least twice that number of their pursuit planes. During that running battle both Lt. de Laage de Meux and Didier Masson shot down Fokker pursuit planes for *Escadrille Américaine.*

Eventually the Nieuports had to break away and return to their emergency fields to refuel and wait for the preassigned time when they were slated to take to the air again. The bombers continued on to the target with the British Royal Naval Air Service Sopwiths leading the way. They went in low over the target and pelted it with their 100-pound bombs. So good was their aim and so effective their bombs that when the French bombers arrived, there was nothing to see but a vast ocean of flame and smoke. They promptly added their tons of bombs to the inferno below and banked around for the flight back home.

By then most of the German planes which had attacked the bombers on their way to the target had landed to refuel and were in the air again. Allied bombers and German pursuits staged a running air battle all the way back to the Rhine River, but not a single bomber was shot out of the air. The escorting Nieuports met the Allied bombers at the Rhine and promptly pitched into the attacking German pursuit planes. Soon more German planes began to drop out of the sky. Neither Lt. de Laage de Meux nor Didier Masson scored in this battle, but Norman Prince shot a Fokker down for his third victory, and Raoul Lufbery also got one for his fifth victory, the one which made him an ace.

By the time the returning bombers were within sight of the French lines the shadows of oncoming night were quickly closing in. The prospect of a possible landing after dark presented no problem to the bomber pilots since they had been trained for both day and night flying. It was a different matter, however, for the pursuit planes. Their pilots were not used to flying at night, and any attempt to land one of the tricky Nieuports in the dark could easily result in a crack-up and fatal injury.

The wisest course of action open to the Nieuport pilots was to open up their throttles wide and speed to their home fields while there was still daylight in the sky. That, though, would have meant leaving the bombers still in enemy controlled air, and open to attack by lurking German planes. Loyal to their original escort assignment, the pursuit pilots stayed on with the squadron until their gas supply ran dangerously low, forcing them to break away one by one and head for the emergency landing field at Corcieux.

Raoul Lufbery and Norman Prince were among those who remained the longest with the bombers. As a matter of fact, all but a few of the bombers had passed over the French lines before low gas tanks made these two pilots turn away toward the emergency landing field. With Lufbery in the lead they flew through the fast-gathering darkness until they sighted the field. After circling it several times Lufbery elected to attempt a landing. He made it without any trouble and taxied his Nieuport off to one side of the field, out of Prince's way.

A few minutes later Prince's Nieuport dropped slowly down, but not from the same direction Lufbery had approached the field. Perhaps in the darkness Prince had become confused; at any rate he came in from the opposite direction—and failed to see a high-tension cable just above some trees that bordered the field.

The Nieuport's landing gear struck the cable, upending the aircraft and sending it plunging nose first into the ground. The

shock of impact broke Prince's safety belt and hurled him a considerable distance from the wrecked plane. Both his legs were broken, and he also received severe internal injuries, but he was still conscious when Lufbery reached him, and suffering terrible pain. His chief concern, though, was not for himself but for other Nieuport pilots headed for the emergency field. He begged Lufbery, and others who had rushed to his aid, to set fire to some cans of gasoline so there would be sufficient light for the other pilots to see the dangerous cable in time.

Lufbery rode in the ambulance with Prince to the hospital. Much of Prince's pain had abated and his broken legs seemed to be the worst of his injuries. The pair told jokes and talked about how soon Prince was likely to return to the squadron, little realizing how seriously he had been injured internally. The next day when Lufbery went to the hospital to visit with Prince he learned that his friend had sunk into a coma. A blood clot had formed in his brain and although the attending doctors exerted all their skills in an effort to relieve it and bring the injured pilot back to consciousness, they met with failure.

Just before Norman Prince died on October 15, 1916, he was promoted to second lieutenant and decorated with France's Legion of Honor. He was buried at Luxeuil with highest military honors, but in 1937 his body was returned to the United States and entombed in a memorial chapel in the National Cathedral in Washington, D.C. As long as men honor the exploits of the Lafayette Flying Corps, Norman Prince will be remembered as its real founder, for it was he who first envisioned the Corps and who did the most to make it a reality.

Two days after Prince's funeral the squadron received orders to move to Cachy-sur-Somme. The Somme front had become a critical area for the Allied high command. Crack ground and air units were being rushed in to defend it against repeated assaults by the German forces. It was a great honor for *Esca-*

drille Américaine to be among the pursuit squadrons assigned to the Somme front, and all the pilots resolved to prove the selection a wise one.

The night before they broke camp the American pilots were given a farewell dinner by the officers of the British Royal Naval Air Service units stationed at the Luxeuil airfield. The British airmen were deeply appreciative of the fine escort job done by the Americans on the Mauser Arms Works bombing raid, and they did their best to make the banquet a memorable affair. Among other things the Americans were loudly toasted by the British as their "Guardian Angels," and the next morning the entire British contingent at Luxeuil turned out to say good-by and wish them well at their new field.

When moving orders for the squadron came through, there were only four of the Nieuports in shape to be flown to the Cachy-sur-Somme field. The rest of the aircraft and all of the squadron's ground equipment were shipped on trucks and other vehicles. The pilots without planes to fly traveled to the new airfield by way of Paris, where they picked up three replacement pilots assigned to the squadron. The new pilots were Willis B. Haviland, of Chicago, Illinois; Frederick H. Prince, of New York, New York, a brother of Norman Prince; and Robert Soubiran, also of New York City.

Bob Soubiran was another of that handful of adventurous Americans who volunteered to fight for France at the outbreak of World War I. He was born of French parents, spoke the language like a native, and like Thaw, Bach, Rockwell, and others, he enlisted in the French Foreign Legion during the very first month of hostilities. He served in the trenches for over a year, and during the Champagne offensive in October, 1915, he was wounded in the knee and hospitalized for four months.

While recuperating in the hospital, Soubiran heard of Norman Prince's idea of forming an all-American squadron to fly under the French colors, and as soon as he returned to his infantry company he applied for and was given a transfer to the French Flying Service. He learned to fly and was breveted a pilot in May, 1916, one month after *Escadrille Américaine* came into existence, but he did not join the squadron until October 22. Before the war Soubiran had done a great deal of automobile racing and was an expert mechanic. Since the French Flying Service badly needed mechanics at the time Soubiran was taught to fly, he was retained at the flight school from May until October to service airplanes instead of being sent to the front to fly and fight with them.

Bob Soubiran's eventual assignment to *Escadrille Américaine* was a fortunate thing for the squadron for two reasons. Not only did he prove himself to be a fine combat pilot, but he was also an enthusiastic amateur photographer who spent practically all his spare time indulging in his hobby. He took pictures of squadron ceremonials, crashes, visiting celebrities, the squadron on the move to a new airfield, and countless shots of the pilots in groups or individually. Without Bob Soubiran and his ever-ready camera, there would have been practically no pictorial record at all of that famous group of American volunteer pilots who flew for France.

In a sense Soubiran's own record of service was practically a complete log of World War I, as far as the experiences of the French and American fighting forces were concerned. For almost eighteen months he fought in the trenches with the Foreign Legion, followed by almost the same length of time with squadrons of the French Flying Service. Then in January, 1918, he was transferred to the U.S. Air Service, in which he served first as flight leader and then as commanding officer of the 103rd Pursuit Squadron until the Armistice was signed on November 11, 1918. After the Armistice he remained in France for another year performing various official duties. One of the first Americans to take up arms for France at the outbreak of the war, Bob Soubiran played an active part until hostilities ended, and was probably one of the last Americans to come home five years later.

When the American pilots arrived at the Cachy-sur-Somme airfield they received one very unpleasant surprise. Up till then they had been living in more or less de luxe quarters, with all kinds of transportation at their disposal, and just about the best food that could be had in war-torn France. But Cachy-sur-Somme was a very different sort of situation.

Instead of a villa or a hotel, they were housed in portable barracks that had been erected in a veritable sea of mud, nine miles from the nearest town. The roofs leaked like sieves, and there were cracks in every wall through which the dank Somme cold seeped, chilling them all to the bone. No blankets had been provided for them, and until they could obtain their own they were forced to sleep in their flying suits. But the crowning blow of all was the fact that the French high command, which had honored them by selecting them for duty on the Somme front, had neglected to make any arrangements for feeding them. When they arrived at Cachy-sur-Somme there was nothing whatever for them to eat, and no future supplies on order.

Fortunately for the American pilots there were, in the area, some French air squadrons whose men generously shared their food with the newcomers until they could make other arrangements. Pooling their ideas and ingenuity, the Lafayette pilots soon solved their problem. A committee was set up with Bill Thaw and Didier Masson in charge, and members took turns driving one of the squadron's small trucks to Paris and bringing it back loaded high with all the food they needed. Another committee took charge of cooking and serving the meals, and still another had the duty of cleaning up. All of the pilots lent a hand in one way or another, and in a very short time they were as comfortable and contented as the cold and rainy late fall Somme climate would allow.

The living conditions at the Cachy-sur-Somme field were one of two entirely new experiences for the pilots of *Escadrille Américaine*. The other was the proximity of the airfield to the actual fighting front. All the other airfields they had been stationed at had been located a considerable distance behind the lines, but not so at the Cachy-sur-Somme airfield. It was so close to the front that the pilots could hear the thunder of the guns and see the lines of observation balloons in the air above both sides of the lines. Often, standing near the barracks, they were able to spot the dirty white puffs of antiaircraft shells exploding high in the air over No Man's Land. The war was now in their front yard, so to speak, and it was their job to help prevent it from coming right into the house!

Chapter
NINE

At the time *Escadrille Américaine* arrived for duty at the Cachy-sur-Somme airfield, the Battle of the Somme was coming to a close. The Somme Blood Bath, as it was to be described in the history books, had been a titanic struggle between combined English and French forces and the Germans for possession of a few miles of bomb-and-shell-torn ground. True, the area fought for, and finally won by the Allies, was of considerable strategic value. But the price paid in dead and wounded was so huge that it dwarfed the significance of the eventual victory.

Two other factors in the Battle of the Somme contributed to making it one of the most crucial engagements in World War I. For the first time in history tanks were used in ground warfare, and although neither side realized it at the time, this battle also marked the end of German superiority in the air.

There were still two more years of ground war to be fought, and countless battles in the sky for mastery of the air. But the German Air Force never again commanded the air as it had at the start of the Battle of the Somme. British and French air squadrons relentlessly cut the Germans down to size while the ground armies locked with each other, and *Escadrille Américaine* did its full share of the job.

Although several of the American pilots were injured or in the hospital, and only about half of the Nieuports in serviceable condition, the squadron still managed to take its regular daily turns patrolling the front lines. Sometimes no more than two or three of the American volunteer pilots were able to fly a patrol, and as a result they often fought air duels with German patrols three and four times their number. Judging by the number of enemy aircraft shot out of the air, *Escadrille Américaine's* tour of duty at Cachy-sur-Somme was perhaps the finest of its entire history. Between October, 1916, and January, 1917, the American pilots boosted their total of confirmed air victories to a figure that ranked them third on the list of French combat squadrons which had shot down the most enemy aircraft.

Another highlight of the squadron's stay at Cachy-sur-Somme was the start of night flying by some of its pilots. Because of the strategic location of the Allied airfield, German aircraft repeatedly bombed it under cover of darkness. At first the American pilots and the French mechanics simply sweated out the nightly German bombing raids in a shelter or slit trench. Eventually, though, they had had enough of cowering in shelters and decided to begin night flying so they could fight back instead of hugging the ground while the enemy bombs fell.

Two of the first to train themselves to fly at night were Lt. de Laage de Meux, the squadron's adjutant, and Paul Pavelka, a replacement pilot from Madison, Connecticut, who had joined *Escadrille Américaine* in August. Like many other Americans, Pavelka had served in the French Foreign Legion until December, 1915, when he obtained his transfer to the French Flying Service, and eventual assignment to *Escadrille Américaine.*

He soon proved himself to be a good pursuit pilot, and although he was never officially credited with having shot down an enemy aircraft, he did make two flights which were to become a part of Lafayette Flying Corps history.

The first was a daylight flight which started off as just another routine patrol over the German lines. After failing to sight a single enemy aircraft, Pavelka was returning to the Cachy-sur-Somme field with gas running low, and had just crossed back over the French lines when suddenly the Nieuport's engine burst into flames. Pavelka had no idea what had caused the fire, but he knew that unless he could somehow put it out, he would be burned alive in the air. As we have mentioned, there were no parachutes in World War I and a pilot either lived or died with his airplane.

Pavelka's only hope was to try and blow out the flames by side-slipping the Nieuport, which he started to do after first switching off the engine. By keeping the nose up and side-slipping first to one side and then to the other, he managed to keep the flames away from his cockpit and the rest of the airplane. But the engine itself kept on burning, and as Pavelka came side-slipping down through the air from ten thousand feet, mounting fear gripped him. Unless he could blow out the fire he would soon be forced to level off and try to land before the flames reached him, or else side-slip straight into the ground.

For the first eight thousand feet of his descent, Pavelka expected the end to come at any moment. Then, at two thousand feet, the flames engulfing the engine suddenly and miraculously died out, and he was able to make a safe dead-stick landing in a field a mile or so behind the French lines. Later when he was telling his squadron mates of his experience, Pavelka stated frankly that it had been far more terrifying than anything he had undergone fighting in the trenches with the French Foreign Legion.

Paul Pavelka's second flight to go down in the annals of the Lafayette Flying Corps occurred when he took off one night from the Cachy-sur-Somme field, accompanied by Lt. de Laage

102

de Meux, to drive off attacking German bombers. Lights had been fitted to the two Nieuports so that they could be quickly identified by the French gunners on the ground, who otherwise might fire on them by mistake. But no sooner had Pavelka taken off into the night sky than his lights went out, and there was nothing he could do to bring them back on.

Ground gunners below heard the sound of his plane, and not being able to see any lights, mistook it for one of the German bombers and opened up a blistering fire. Luckily none of their bullets touched Pavelka's plane, but since he was unable to signal in any way that his was a friendly aircraft, the only thing he could do was to climb for more and more altitude and try to spot one of the German bombers in the dark sky.

Although he was able to see certain sections of the ground clearly enough to be able to tell where he was all the time, he did not catch sight of a single enemy aircraft. Once or twice he thought he saw the faint glow of an airplane engine's exhaust, but when he raced his Nieuport across to the spot there was nothing there.

As he flew around, well out of the range of the ground guns, he also searched for the fixed lights on Lt. de Laage de Meux's Nieuport. He failed to spot them because the squadron adjutant's airplane was no longer in the air. Five minutes after take-off, Lt. de Laage de Meux's engine quit cold on him and he had been forced to make a hasty dead-stick landing on the edge of the airfield while the Germans were still bombing it. Fortunately neither he nor his plane were hit by flying bomb fragments.

Eventually Paul Pavelka gave up chasing phantoms in the dark sky and decided to go down and land on the Cachy-sur-Somme field. He could no longer see the flash of bombs bursting below and guessed that the Germans had completed their raid and were now on the way home, leaving him all by himself. Sliding down toward his own home field, he fully expected that when those on the field heard his engine they would light the oil pot flares for him to land by. But it did not work out that way.

Those on the ground heard his engine all right, but they believed it to be the engine of a German plane sneaking back for one more bombing run. All the ground guns opened up full blast, filling the air about Pavelka's plane with hissing bullets as he banked away in a hurry. Gaining altitude and getting clear of the guns, he tried to reach the field from a different direction. But as soon as those on the ground heard him coming down, they once more opened up blindly on the area of night sky from which the sound of his engine came.

Again and again Pavelka tried to slip down and land, but each time the blasting fire of the ground guns forced him back up for altitude. What he did not know was that the entire area had been alerted to be on guard for "a lone enemy plane sneaking about in the night sky," and orders issued to shoot it down if at all possible.

Of course the ground gunners could not actually see him in the dark, and could only aim their guns in the direction of the sound of the Nieuport's engine. But Pavelka was to say later that more than a few of those blindly fired bullets came much too close to his plane for comfort. At any rate they drove him farther and farther away from the Cachy-sur-Somme field, and eventually there was little more than a cupful of gas left in his tank.

Fortunately for him he had taken off on his wild night-flying mission long after midnight, and when his gas supply ran dangerously low there was enough dawn light coming out of the east to eliminate the danger of a night landing on unfamiliar ground. He glided down and managed to land safely

and undisturbed in a field some *forty* miles from Cachy-sur-Somme, near a small town called Martainville. Pavelka said later that he had never been so happy to be back on solid ground. Bad luck, however, was still with him. Before he could obtain gas for his plane, foul weather closed in on the area and three days passed before he was able to fly back to Cachy-sur-Somme and rejoin his squadron.

Two months later Paul Pavelka said good-by to his flying mates in *Escadrille Américaine*. Wanting to see action on all the fronts of the war, he requested a transfer to a French pursuit squadron operating on the Salonika front in the Mediterranean theater of operations. There death awaited him, but not from a bullet or a shell or a bomb. Shortly after arriving on the Salonika front he made friends with some British cavalry officers stationed there. Having been an ardent horseman all his life, he begged his British friends to let him ride a particular horse well known for being vicious and almost unmanageable. During the ride the horse fell and rolled on Pavelka, causing internal injuries from which he never recovered. He died on November 17, 1917, and was buried with full military honors by his French squadron flying mates and officers of the British cavalry regiment stationed near the airfield.

At about the time Paul Pavelka made his wild night flight against the German planes bombing the Cachy-sur-Somme airfield, two events were taking place—one in Washington, D.C., the other in Paris—which were directly to affect the history of *Escadrille Américaine* N. 124.

During the fall of 1916 the exploits and accomplishments of *Escadrille Américaine* were receiving world-wide publicity. Almost every day the United States newspapers carried a glowing account of some Lafayette pilot's daring feat. Bill Thaw, Raoul Lufbery, and some of the others had become national heros. From Maine to California people were stirred by what a small group of daring American volunteer pilots was doing in a war far from their native shores.

Frankly, some of the newspaper and magazine stories written about the American pilots were greatly exaggerated, and a few even downright fictitious. Had they known at the time what was being written about them back home, the *Escadrille Américaine* pilots would undoubtedly have been the first to deny the fantastic accounts of their efforts. However, they were too busy helping to fight a war, and were completely unaware of what was being written and said of them thousands of miles away.

The French Government was of course very much pleased by the fame attained by *Escadrille Américaine* in the United States. One of the main reasons official permission had been granted for the formation of such a squadron was the French Government's hope that it would arouse interest in the neutral United States and sympathy for the French cause. And that was exactly what had happened. Millions of Americans read about the *Escadrille Américaine,* and as a result more and more of them became annoyed at their country's continued rigid neutrality stand. More and more men, too, followed in the footsteps of that first group of American volunteers and enlisted in the armed services of France.

The other side of the picture, however, was entirely different. The German Government was enraged by the wide publicity being given *Escadrille Américaine.* In November of 1916 the German ambassador at Washington, D.C., Count Johann Heinrich von Bernstorff, officially protested to the United States Government that a number of Americans, citizens of a neutral country, were fighting for France against Germany. Oddly enough the German ambassador's protest made no mention of the fact that quite a number of Americans were also fighting in the ranks of the British and Canadian armed forces. Perhaps, though, it was simply because those Americans were more or less unknown and received little coverage in the American press.

The American Government, still anxious to maintain a stand of strict neutrality in the European conflict, reacted quickly to the German protest and sent a note to the French Ministry of War in Paris. The contents of that note have never been released. In fact, as far as can be determined, the note never became a part of official United States Government records. However, on November 16, 1916, Dr. Edmund L. Gros, head of the American Field Service and a ranking member of the committee originally organized to persuade the French Government to permit the forming of an all-American air squadron, received a startling communication from Colonel Barres, Chief of the French Flying Service. It stated that *Escadrille Américaine* was no longer to be called by that name. Instead it was to be known simply as *Escadrille* N. 124.

Dr. Gros was stunned by the news. He went to see Colonel Barres and was told about the protest by the German ambassador in Washington, D.C., and of the note the United States Government had sent to the French Government. He was also shown a more recent letter from the French Ministry of War to French General Headquarters stating that for diplomatic reasons *Escadrille Américaine* was henceforth to be known as *Escadrille des Volontaires,* and that the commanding officer of the 13th Combat Group was to be notified immediately of the French Ministry of War's order.

The order to change the squadron's name was a terrific blow to the morale of the American pilots. But what angered them most was that the new name (Squadron of Volunteers) did not in any way indicate it was an air combat squadron made up of American pilots. It was a known fact that many men of various nationalities were fighting with the French armed forces. In the early months of the war there were even some eight hundred men of German birth who fought in the French Foreign Legion against their own country. To the outside world a French air squadron called *Escadrille des Volontaires* might very well be thought to consist of many different nationalities, when in truth it was completely American.

Dr. Gros and other members of the committee protested vigorously against the squadron change of name. The pilots themselves also protested, and after much discussion the name *Escadrille des Volontaires* was vetoed and the name Lafayette Escadrille suggested in its place. To Bill Thaw goes the credit for thinking up the new name in honor of the Marquis de Lafayette who, one hundred and thirty-eight years before, had volunteered his services to the American colonists in their war against England for independence.

The French Government was pleased that the American pilots wished to name their squadron after so great a Frenchman and soon agreed to the new name, which became official in November of 1916.

At about the same time the name of the *Escadrille Américaine* was being changed, another name change was being made in Paris. As a result, the recently formed Franco-American Flying Corps became the Lafayette Flying Corps.

After *Escadrille Américaine* N. 124 had served several months at the front and had begun to make a name for itself, the committee that had helped gain French backing for it realized that other American youths back in the United States would soon be wanting to volunteer to fly and fight for France. However, wanting to volunteer wouldn't be enough; new recruits would also need money for boat fare to France and more money to live on until they were accepted for flight training.

To help solve this problem, the original committee established the Franco-American Flying Corps and set up offices in Paris to handle the finances and other business of the Corps. A Countess Greffulhe donated a building at 15 Avenue des Champs Élysées for use as Corps headquarters, and it quickly became a home away from home for all American volunteers whenever they were in Paris.

From the Paris offices of the Franco-American Flying Corps money was provided for American youths still in the States who wanted to volunteer to fly for France but did not have the price of the trans-Atlantic boat fare.

After a prospective volunteer had been passed upon by the Corps representative in New York City, he was given his fare to France; and as soon as he reached Paris he reported to the Corps' offices for a medical examination. He was then sent to the French Bureau of Recruiting in *Les Invalides* building. There he signed the papers for enlistment in the French Foreign Legion, but was immediately given his transfer papers to the French Flying Service.

It was, of course, impossible for the Executive Committee of the Franco-American Flying Corps to know for sure that a volunteer would successfully complete his flight school training and be breveted a pilot. To cover this eventuality a special arrangement was made with the French Government to the effect that if any American volunteer failed to graduate from flying school, he would be given his outright release from the French Flying Service and not, as was the case with French enlistees, be transferred to some other branch of the French armed forces.

Each volunteer who did graduate from flight school was presented with a uniform by the Franco-American Flying Corps, and provided with money for personal expenses if he required it. He was also given an allowance while serving at the front to supplement the meager French Flying Service pay.

The money paid out by the Paris offices of the Franco-

American Flying Corps was obtained from donations by interested people on both sides of the Atlantic. One of the most enthusiastic and important supporters was William K. Vanderbilt of New York City, whose donations alone eventually totaled over five hundred thousand francs.

Although the Franco-American Flying Corps became the Lafayette Flying Corps at about the same time the name *Escadrille Américaine* was changed to the Lafayette Escadrille, there is no record that this was also done at the request of the French Government. Perhaps Dr. Gros and other members of the Executive Committee in Paris decided on the name change to avoid any of the unpleasantness that had occurred when the French Government ordered the *Escadrille Américaine* to change its name. Changing the name did avoid any further unpleasantness, but it also created a misunderstanding by millions of people back in the United States—one that continued to exist long after the war was over.

The misunderstanding was natural enough, since the two names sounded so much alike, and many people assumed that a Lafayette Flying Corps pilot flew with the Lafayette Escadrille. Such was *not* the case, for a very simple and obvious reaon. The French word *escadrille* means squadron, and a French air squadron in World War I was made up of from only twelve to fifteen pilots. The Lafayette Escadrille never had more than fifteen pilots on its roster at any one time, and any replacement pilot sent to the squadron merely took the place of some veteran pilot who had been killed, or wounded, or otherwise removed from active flying.

In other words, the Lafayette Escadrille was simply the name of the all-American squadron flying under the French colors, and was not composed of *all* the pilots in the Lafayette Flying Corps. As a matter of fact, of the one hundred and eighty volunteer Americans who saw action at the front in the French Flying

Service during World War I, only thirty-eight served with the Lafayette Escadrille. The rest were posted to other French air squadrons because there was no room for them in the Lafayette Escadrille at the time they received their pilot's wings. But all one hundred and eighty pilots were members of the Lafayette Flying Corps—and more than a few who did not actually serve with the Lafayette Escadrille racked up impressive records of their own and became leading air aces.

Chapter
TEN

The French 13th Combat Group at the Somme front consisted of five crack pursuit squadrons, of which Lafayette Escadrille N. 124 was one. During most of the 1916–1917 winter the entire Group was flying the Nieuport 27, but in late January, just before the Group moved to Saint Just on the Oise front, two or three of the squadrons were equipped with the brand-new Spad pursuit plane. The letters S-P-A-D stood for the manufacturer's name, *Societé pour l'Aviation et des Dérivés.*

The Spad, which eventually became the most famous airplane in World War I with the exception of the British Sopwith Camel, was a biplane powered with a 150-horsepower water-cooled Hispano-Suiza engine. The first model of the Spad, however, was not fitted with radiator shutters to make warming up before take-off a simple and speedy process. As a result, on many occasions the pilots of the Lafayette Escadrille, not yet fitted out with Spads, flew emergency patrols which normally would have been flown by a Spad squadron if the pilots had been able to warm up their engines faster.

Later on, shutters were fitted to the Spad's Hispano-Suiza engine and the warming-up problem was completely solved. By the middle of 1917 all French pursuit squadrons were equipped with the Spad, but the Lafayette Escadrille was one of the last to receive the new plane. It was, however, no strange aircraft to the American pilots. In December of 1916 Bill Thaw went to Paris to pick up a new Spad and fly it back to the squadron so that his fellow pilots could make practice flights and be thoroughly familiar with its flying characteristics by the time the squadron changed over to that type of aircraft.

Besides picking up a Spad, Thaw had a second, more unusual reason for making that trip to Paris. Whiskey, the squadron mascot lion cub, had injured an eye and Thaw took him along to have it treated by a veterinarian. Unfortunately, though, each veterinarian Thaw took Whiskey to was scared off by the lion cub's ferocious roars. But Thaw did accomplish one thing for Whiskey's benefit on the trip; he obtained a companion for him, a female lion cub whom the pilots named Soda. Soda was never as playful with the pilots as Whiskey, but the two cubs became very fond of each other. They remained almost inseparable until that day in 1918 when the U.S. Air Service took over the Lafayette Escadrille, and it became the U.S. 103rd Aero Squadron. By then Whiskey and Soda had grown to almost full size and the American brass hats wanted no part of them on an Air Service airfield. So Whiskey and Soda were given to a Paris zoo, and whenever any of the former Lafayette Escadrille pilots were in the French capital on leave, they always went to the zoo to say hello to their one-time squadron mascots.

Although the 1916–1917 winter weather slowed down ground warfare considerably, the air war continued at its usual furious pace. The German air squadrons fought savagely to regain mastery of the air on the Somme front, while the Lafayette Escadrille, together with the other squadrons of the 13th Combat Group, fought just as savagely to retain control. By the end of January, when the Lafayette Escadrille moved to Saint

Just on the Oise front, its pilots had racked up an officially confirmed total of twenty-eight enemy planes shot down and destroyed.

Just before the move to Saint Just the Lafayette Escadrille received three new replacement pilots: Edwin C. Parsons, of Springfield, Massachusetts; Edmond Genêt, of Ossining, New York; and Ronald W. Hoskier, of South Orange, New Jersey.

Ted Parsons, like Clyde Balsley before him, was truly a fashion plate—the perfect example of what the well-dressed airman should wear. When on leave in Paris or at some 13th Combat Group ceremonial, Parsons might have seemed only a picture book aviator, but in the air he was a bold and skilled fighter, and as deadly a shot as the next man.

Despite his impeccable appearance Parsons had never been in really good physical shape. As a youth his tonsils gave him considerable trouble, one of his eyelids continually twitched, and he lost the little finger on his left hand as the result of an infection. He frequently suffered respiratory trouble, and in addition he was slightly color-blind.

Suffering from so many afflictions, Parsons could easily have elected to stay out of the war—at least until his own country became one of the combatants. However, he was one of those adventurous types who thrived on excitement and danger, and in 1915 he worked his way to France. When he arrived he tried to enlist in the French Flying Service, but it was before the rule barring foreign enlistments was changed and he was told to try the French Foreign Legion. Because of his poor health, Parsons was afraid he wouldn't be able to last very long in that rough, tough fighting unit, so instead he enlisted in the American Field Service.

For several months he drove an ambulance on the Soissons front, and then on April 13, 1916, he obtained his release from the Field Service and presented himself at the recruiting offices of the French Flying Service. As luck would have it, or because the French were at that time desperately in need of pilots, he passed his physical examination and was sent to an air school for flight training. In August of 1916 he was breveted a pilot, and in January, 1917, he was assigned to the Lafayette Escadrille at Cachy-sur-Somme. He remained with the all-American squadron until February 26, 1918, and although he did more than his share of patrol flying and fought countless air battles with the Germans, he was not officially credited with a single enemy plane shot down.

When the Lafayette Escadrille was taken over by the U.S. Air Service and became the 103rd Pursuit Squadron, Parsons was one of several Americans flying in a French uniform who did not care to transfer to the U.S. Air Service. He elected to remain with the French, whom he had come to respect and highly admire, and was sent to the Stork Squadron with which the famed Capt. Georges Guynemer had flown. Parsons remained with the Storks until the end of the war and was officially credited with shooting down seven German aircraft.

Ronald W. Hoskier, another of the new squadron replacements, was regarded as the baby of the Lafayette Escadrille because he was the youngest of all the pilots. But from the very start Hoskier displayed a man's maturity and judgment when he was piloting his plane in tricky, demanding situations. Hoskier's story is unique because he happened to be traveling in France with his father and mother during the summer of 1914, and when war broke out the whole family went to the aid of the French cause. His father, Herman C. Hoskier, became a member of the Norton-Harjes Ambulance Service, a voluntary Franco-American group; his mother became a nurse in a Paris military hospital; and young Hoskier joined the American Field Service.

By April, 1916, the lure of the air had taken a firm grip on

Ron Hoskier, and a month later he enlisted in the French Flying Service. He became a pilot in December of the same year, and in January, 1917, he was assigned to the Lafayette Escadrille. Although he was the squadron "infant" he soon earned the respect of all the veteran pilots. The squadron's adjutant, Lt. de Laage de Meux, took a particular liking to him and they became exceptionally close friends. Both were men of refinement, culture, and more than average intelligence—but their friendship was destined to be of short duration.

In April, 1917, the Lafayette Escadrille was still a Nieuport 27 squadron, but it had received two of the new Spads and also a two-seater Morane Parasol. The Parasol was not an official combat plane of the squadron. It was simply an extra aircraft it had somehow obtained, and on occasion one of the pilots would make a reconnaissance patrol in it with a French corporal, Jean Dressy, in the rear cockpit as machine gunner. Corporal Dressy was Lt. de Laage de Meux's orderly, and on April 23, 1917, Ron Hoskier and the corporal took the Morane Parasol up for a flight which turned out to be the last one either of them ever made.

The two men flew behind the German lines to determine the effect of a recent French artillery barrage. Bill Thaw and two other pilots went along in their Nieuports as a fighter escort. They climbed in formation to an altitude of seven thousand feet where they leveled off and started across No Man's Land. No sooner had they reached the German lines, however, than they ran into a patrol of six enemy planes. After signaling to Hoskier and Corporal Dressy to continue toward their objective, Thaw and the two others dived on the German aircraft.

Unfortunately, though, before Thaw and the two other Nieuport pilots could get within shooting range, the German planes slid into a thick cloud bank. The three Americans plowed into the cloud bank after them, but were unable to flush them out into clear air. When they finally came out themselves they started searching the skies for sight of Hoskier and Corporal Dressy, but they were never to see either of them alive again.

Exactly what happened to the two has remained a mystery through the years, but at the time it was believed Hoskier had sighted a German plane and fearlessly attacked it with the old two-seater Parasol. At any rate, a short time afterward a French balloon observer reported having seen a lone Morane Parasol ringed by German pursuit planes and being riddled with bullets. The two in the doomed Parasol had fought back to the last, but they didn't stand a chance. The wings of the Parasol suddenly came off and the fuselage dropped to earth like a rock. It struck on the French side of the lines and the two smashed bodies in the wreckage were identified as those of Ron Hoskier and Corporal Dressy. They were buried side by side with full military honors.

Edmond Genêt, the third replacement to join the Lafayette Escadrille in that January of 1917, was the great-great-grandson of the French ambassador to the United States in 1793. The ambassador's name was also Edmond Genêt, but he was to become better known in history as Citizen Genêt. When he was eventually recalled by his government, his political party was not in power in France, and he refused to return to his native country. Instead, he bought a farm on Long Island, New York, and became an American citizen.

When World War I broke out in 1914, young Edmond Genêt was filled with the desire to go to France and help fight for the country of his forefathers. But several things prevented him from acting on his wish. He was only eighteen years old, and a person had to be twenty-one to obtain a passport. And he also happened to be a seaman in the United States Navy!

His ambition to fight for France didn't lessen with the passing of time, however, and early in 1915 he did something about it. He went to New York, lied about his age, and obtained a passport. Then, without so much as a note to the U.S. Navy to say that he was quitting the service, he set sail for France and enlisted in the French Foreign Legion. Two months later he was fighting in the trenches and winning high praise for his courage and daring under fire.

Because of his small size, he was affectionately called Little Genêt, first by his Foreign Legion comrades, and later by his flying mates. He saw sixteen months of front-line service with the Foreign Legion, but by May of 1916 his ambition had switched to the skies. He obtained his transfer to the French Flying Service, and at flight school he set one of the best training records of any American who flew for France.

Learning to fly and winning his wings was almost an obsession with Genêt, and when a bad crash sent him to the hospital it was all the doctors and nurses could do to keep him there until he was fully recovered from his injuries. Finally, in September, 1916, he was breveted a pilot, and in January of 1917 he joined the Lafayette Escadrille.

When Little Genêt reached the front he seemed to live only for flying. Like Victor Chapman, he was almost always in the air on a patrol whether it was his turn or not. More than once his flying mates pleaded with him to take it easy lest he wear himself out, but the scrappy little air fighter paid no heed to their advice and continued to fly as long as there was gas in his tank and light to see by.

Then on April 16, 1917, he flew his last patrol.

Raoul Lufbery and he took off together that day to scout some German troop movements. Low-hanging clouds forced them to fly only a thousand or so feet above the ground, and as a result, German antiaircraft batteries were able to open up on them at almost point-blank range when they reached the enemy side of No Man's Land. The whole sky about them be-

119

came peppered by ugly gray shell bursts and the two light Nieuports were rocked about like ships on a turbulent sea.

While they were still under heavy fire, Lufbery happened to glance over at Genêt's plane just in time to see it go curving around as though its pilot were heading it back toward his home field. On impuse Lufbery banked his own Nieuport around just in case Genêt was in some kind of trouble. A few moments later, though, Genêt's Nieuport slid into some low-hanging clouds and disappeared. Lufbery went in after him but when he came out again, Genêt was nowhere to be seen.

Believing that Genêt had somehow outdistanced him and was well on his way back to their home airfield, Lufbery turned toward German-held territory once more and completed his reconnaissance patrol. When he finally returned to the Lafayette Escadrille's airfield, he learned that Genêt had not landed there. He must either have lost his way back or else been forced to land at another field because of engine trouble or some other difficulty. An hour or so later, though, a telephone call from a French infantry command post revealed the sad truth. The infantrymen had seen Little Genêt's plane fall to earth and crash at a point just inside the French lines. When some of the Lafayette Escadrille pilots reached the spot, Genêt's smashed body was still in the wreckage. Examination of the plane later proved that a direct hit by a German antiaircraft shell had killed Little Genêt instantly and sent the Nieuport flying into the ground with its engine wide open.

Edmond Genêt's flying record with the Lafayette Escadrille was one of the best. And he was also the first volunteer American pilot flying for France to die in action *after* the United States entered World War I.

The last volunteer American pilot in French uniform to die in action *before* the United States entered the war was James McConnell. Incidentally, he was also the fourth and last of the original seven members of *Escadrille Américaine* N. 124 to give his life for France.

Jim McConnell was different in many ways from the six other original members of *Escadrille Américaine*. Neither a cosmopolitan like Bill Thaw and Raoul Lufbery, nor an adventurer like Kiffin Rockwell, Victor Chapman, and Norman Prince, McConnell was simply an average American—reasonably intelligent, even-tempered, responsible in his actions, and a lover of sports.

He was what was known as a pilots' pilot—a man who did his job day in and day out, took the bad breaks and the good ones in stride, and never complained or talked about himself. A perfect example of his character and ability is contained in the story of one of his countless patrols over the German lines. While returning from this particular patrol his engine quit cold on him and he was forced to make a dead-stick landing behind the French lines. Unfortunately, he had to land in some pretty rugged terrain and cracked up his airplane. Although he escaped serious injury he did wrench his back severely. He was in almost constant pain, but he made no mention of it and continued to fly his share of the patrols until finally, unable to walk, he was shipped off to a military hospital.

Anxious to get back to the squadron, he daily pestered the doctors for permission to leave the hospital. Eventually they granted his request, not knowing that rheumatism had settled in his back, and that even the slightest movement filled him with pain. But when he returned to the squadron and started taking his turn flying patrols, his stiff, obviously painful movements became very evident to his flying mates. They begged him to go back into the hospital and receive further medical treatment, but he insisted he was perfectly all right and kept on flying. A week after his release from the military hospital Jim McConnell flew his last patrol.

The date was March 19, 1917, and McConnell was scheduled to fly on reconnaissance with Ted Parsons and Edmond (Little) Genêt. Shortly before take-off, though, Parsons had trouble with his engine and was forced to withdraw from the patrol. McConnell and Genêt took off together and crossed over the lines heading for their ground objective in the Saint Quentin sector. Suddenly they spotted two German Albatros two-seaters a couple of thousand feet below, and they both dived immediately on the enemy planes.

There were fairly thick cloud banks that day on both sides of the lines, and the German pilots, seeing the two French Nieuports diving on them, headed quickly for the safety of the nearest one. McConnell and Genêt went in together after them, but when Genêt came out into clear air again he found himself alone. Although McConnell was nowhere to be seen, one of the Albatros two-seaters was banking away in front of him. Genêt gave chase, but before he could bring his aerial machine gun to bear on the Albatros, its pilot whipped it around and opened fire on him. Despite the great range a lucky bullet hit one of Genêt's wing struts and the ricocheting pieces struck him in the face.

The bits of shattered bullet just barely cut Genêt's cheek and he was able to continue after the Albatros. However, it soon ducked into some clouds again and he lost track of it. Genêt gave up the pursuit and spent some time looking for Jim McConnell. Unable to locate him in the cloud-filled sky, he eventually turned back toward his home airfield, expecting to find that McConnell had returned ahead of him. But McConnell was not there. As the hours dragged on, Genêt waited with the other pilots of the squadron for some sign of McConnell's returning Nieuport or some word from him. But none came.

Several days later French troops found a wrecked Nieuport near the front lines. It was McConnell's, and his dead body lay

amid the wreckage. A peasant woman who lived nearby said that she had seen McConnell's Nieuport fighting with a German plane when suddenly a second German plane had joined the fight. Seconds later McConnell's Nieuport fell off on one wing and went plummeting down to the ground. Thus died the last Lafayette pilot before the United States entered the war, a man who had written in his diary the night before his death, "This war may kill me, but I have it to thank for much."

There were sorrowful days for the pilots of the Lafayette Escadrille in the spring of 1917, but there were also days of aerial triumph and grim satisfaction. In its first year at the front the all-American squadron had set a record of which all its members could be justly proud. The squadron had flown over four hundred combat and reconnaissance patrols, most of them deep into German-held air. A total of thirty-three enemy planes had been shot down and officially confirmed, and at least twice that number had been destroyed too far behind the German lines to receive official confirmation. The price the squadron had paid was nine pilots killed in action, five too severely wounded to remain at the front, and a dozen others so exhausted by constant service in the air that they had to be sent to rest camps and replaced by pilots fresh from flying school

All in all the squadron's first-year record was a truly splendid accomplishment, but it was little more than the beginning. There were still to be many more months of victory, and of death, too, for the pilots of the Lafayette Escadrille in the skies above war-torn France.

Chapter

ELEVEN

All during the spring of 1917 the pilots of the Lafayette Escadrille continued to battle it out with their German adversaries, and more often than not they came off the victors. But they were not the only volunteer American pilots who were making a name for themselves in the air. Serving with other French air squadrons were the Lafayette Flying Corps pilots, for whom there had been no room in the Lafayette Escadrille when they graduated from flight school. Two of these pilots—Frank L. Baylies and David Putnam—were eventually credited with destroying more enemy planes in aerial combat than any other Lafayette pilot with the exception of Raoul Lufbery. Baylies and Putnam each scored twelve confirmed air victories, as against Raoul Lufbery's seventeen.

Frank Baylies came from New Bedford, Massachusetts. A well-built youth, although a bit on the stocky side, he was a topflight performer in all kinds of sports. In everything Baylies attempted, perfection was his goal, and it was undoubtedly that driving ambition to be the best that later helped him become one of the Lafayette's greatest aces.

In February of 1916 Baylies sailed for France and enlisted

in the American Field Service. He saw a year of almost constant duty on the various fronts, and his high courage under fire earned him the French *Croix de Guerre with Palm*. A month after the United States entered the war in 1917, Baylies obtained his transfer from the Field Service to the French Flying Service.

At the flight training schools at Pau and at Avord he proved himself to be an exceptionally brilliant student, inspiring one of his instructors to remark that "he has the true touch of a pilot." Baylies was also apparently oblivious to the dangers of flying, and on one occasion when his instructor was busy with other students he took an old Blériot monoplane aloft and put it through a maneuver that was regarded as almost certain death in that type of airplane. While flying high over the airfield he turned the Blériot into a spinning nose dive and dropped down to an altitude of only a couple of thousand feet before pulling the airplane out of the spin and making a perfect landing. (In World War I there were many, many pilots, both in training and at the front, who were killed because they were unable to pull their airplane out of a spinning nose dive, and spun right on down into the ground.)

Frank Baylies was breveted in September of 1917 and was sent to a French Spad squadron because there was no room on the Lafayette Escadrille pilot roster. He served with that Spad squadron for a month and then was sent to Capt. Georges Guynemer's famous Stork squadron. At the time the Storks were patrolling the skies over Noyon, Montdidier, and the Somme. Almost every day they engaged in aerial battles with pilots from some of Germany's crack pursuit units which had recently been sent to those important fronts.

For a pilot with as little front-line flying experience as Baylies had, such tough, seasoned enemy opposition could have made a nervous wreck of him—if not worse. But Baylies took

126

it in stride as all a part of the day's work. What he lacked in experience he more than made up for in daring, uncanny flying skill, steady nerves, and an almost unbelievably accurate aim with an aerial machine gun. His flying and fighting tactics were absolutely faultless, and once he attacked an enemy plane he fought relentlessly until the enemy either got away from him or went hurtling to earth in flames. Although for some unknown reason it was never recorded officially, within five weeks after joining the Storks, Frank Baylies shot down five German planes, all of which were confirmed, and he became an ace.

A good example of Baylies' dogged qualities as an air fighter is found in the story of one of his countless patrols over the enemy lines. He had been patrolling for half an hour in apparently empty skies when he spotted a lone German plane far behind its own lines. He immediately gave chase, and because of his Spad's greater speed he presently caught up with the German and charged in to attack. The German hurled his plane all over the sky in a frantic effort to keep clear of Baylies' fire. For a while he successfully eluded Baylies' bullets and at the same time managed to get closer and closer to the safety of the ground below. Baylies followed him all the way down, however, and not until a burst from his machine gun had sent the German aircraft hurtling in flames the rest of the short distance to the ground did he pull out of his final wild dive and head back toward the French lines.

Flying so low, he made an especially vulnerable target for the German antiaircraft guns. They peppered him relentlessly as he streaked over the ground, and why he and his plane were not blasted out of the air is a mystery. Baylies' good fortune didn't last the whole distance, however. As he was nearing the French lines a burst of ground fire ripped open the sump of the Spad's engine. All the engine's oil drained out, and in a matter of seconds the overheated Hispano-Suiza engine stopped cold.

127

Because of the low altitude, the only thing Baylies could do was to try and stretch his glide enough to reach the safety of French-held ground just ahead. But that was a tricky thing to do with a French Spad.

With most World War I planes the pilot could flatten out the angle of glide to a point where the plane was losing only a minimum of altitude and could still be kept under control. Not so with the Spad. It was so heavy for its size that it had hardly any gliding angle at all, and once the engine was shut off it practically dropped to the ground. Fliers nicknamed the Spad The Flying Brick, and the best way to land it was to bring the plane down to within a few feet of the ground and then throttle back and let it drop the rest of the way. The tail skid of the Spad was two or three times the thickness of any other pursuit plane's tail skid, and for good reason. When the Spad's tail came down on landing it hit against the ground hard enough to splinter any ordinary tail skid.

Aware of these drawbacks, Baylies employed every bit of his flying skill to stretch out the Spad's glide, and even then he did not quite make it all the way to safety. Gravity took over completely when he was halfway between the French and German trenches, and he touched down in No Man's Land. Realizing that he was not going to reach the French lines, Baylies had unsnapped his safety belt before the touchdown and stood up on the seat. As the Spad started to bounce and swerve crazily over the shell-pocked ground he leaped out and ran at full speed for the French trenches. With German soldiers in the opposite trenches shooting at him, he zigzagged this way and that until he was able to dive headlong into the first French trench. Shortly afterward, German artillery opened up on the spot where his Spad had flopped over on its back in No Man's Land. By the time the fire died down and French soldiers were able to escort Baylies back to where he could get transportation to his airfield, there was nothing left of his Spad but matchwood and shredded fabric.

During the four months Frank Baylies served with the Storks, he racked up twelve officially confirmed air victories and probably twice as many unconfirmed ones. Then, on March 17, 1918, he dueled in the air with the enemy for the last time. The encounter took place at about five o'clock in the afternoon in the sky between the French towns of Crèvecoeur and Lassigny, and there were several different, conflicting accounts of what happened.

Ted Parsons, who had been with another French Spad squadron since leaving the Lafayette Escadrille when the U.S. Air Service took it over, was in the air at the time and reported seeing a French Spad with Stork Squadron markings mixing it up with a lone German plane. Suddenly four more German planes had swooped down out of the high sky to join in the fight, and eventually the French Spad went down in flames.

Another Lafayette Flying Corps pilot, Reginald Sinclaire, of Corning, New York, who was with the French Spad Squadron No. 68, also reported seeing Frank Baylies' last air battle, but gave quite a different account. According to Sinclaire, he and another pilot of his squadron were flying a reconnaissance patrol when they sighted a patrol of German Fokkers flying high some distance behind the enemy lines. Cutting short their patrol, they headed for the Fokkers to engage them in battle. As they flew through the air at full throttle they saw three French Spads with the Stork Escadrille insignia on the fuselage giving chase to a flight of German triplanes. Shortly after the Fokkers they were chasing ducked from sight into a cloud bank, Sinclaire and his squadron companion saw one of the Stork Spads go hurtling to earth in flames.

Whether the Spad Ted Parsons reported seeing going down in flames, or the one Reginald Sinclaire saw, was piloted by

Frank Baylies was never determined because neither Baylies' body nor his wrecked plane was ever found.

The other American volunteer pilot who never flew with the Lafayette Escadrille, but who made Lafayette Flying Corps history all the same, was David Putnam, an all-round athlete from Brookline, Massachusetts.

In the spring of 1917 American newspapers were full of stories about the Lafayette Escadrille in far-off France, and Raoul Lufbery became David Putnam's idol. Putnam was a student at Harvard at the time, but he left school before the spring semester ended, driven by a strong urge to become a flier and participate in the action and adventure he'd been reading about. Apparently unaware that there was a Lafayette Flying Corps recruiting office in New York City, Putnam worked his way to France on a cattle boat. When he arrived in France he enlisted in the French Flying Service, and on May 31 he was sent to flying school at Avord to begin his training on the Blériot monoplane.

After he completed his preliminary training at Avord he went to school at Pau for further instruction. While there he established himself as one of the most brilliant students who ever attended that advanced flight training school. Long before he reached the front his instructors were saying that he was a born pilot.

On December 12, 1917, Dave Putnam joined the French Spad No. 94 Squadron, and he received his baptism of fire over the enemy lines on the 22nd of the same month. He did not destroy any German planes during the five weeks he flew with Spad No. 94, but his brilliant flying and daring battle tactics convinced his superior officers that he was a pilot of great merit. After being transferred from Spad No. 94 to French Escadrille No. 156, Putnam started to prove his superiors right in their estimation of him by shooting down his first German plane in only a matter of seconds.

Escadrille No. 156 was equipped with the newly designed Morane Parasol pursuit plane, the smallest, fastest, and most highly maneuverable of all the French pursuit planes. It was often referred to as the Hornet, and with Dave Putnam at the controls it must have really seemed like an angry, stinging hornet to those German pilots who were unlucky enough to meet it in the air.

Once he had downed his first confirmed German plane, Putnam became a terror of the skies, as far as enemy pilots were concerned. No matter how great the odds against him, he was always on the attack. On one occasion he took on singlehandedly a formation of four German planes and fought them all over the sky for no less than thirty-five minutes. For a dogfight of one against four to last that long was almost incredible, but performing the incredible was common practice with Dave Putnam. What's more, he not only fought the four Germans for thirty-five minutes, but in the end he shot one of them down and forced the other three to flee for safety.

As if fighting four Germans alone was just a warm-up, Putnam on the following day tackled a flight of eight enemy planes and sent two of them flaming to earth. And shortly after that, he dived on an entire German squadron, consisting of *eighteen* planes, shot down the leader and got safely away. Almost overnight he became an air ace with five enemy victories officially credited to him, and no one knows how many others destroyed, but unseen by Allied eyes.

On June 1, 1918, Dave Putnam was transferred to the French Spad Squadron No. 38. Spad No. 38 was commanded by Capt. Georges Félix Madon, one of France's most famous combat pilots, a man officially credited with shooting down forty-one German planes. Captain Madon saw instantly in Putnam the makings of a truly great pilot, and took him under his wing to teach him all the ins and outs of successful air fighting.

Just five days later, on June 5, Putnam put what Captain Madon had taught him into practice and succeeded in doing something that no more than four or five other pilots, friend and foe, had attempted in all the years of World War I. While flying alone Putnam attacked a German formation of twelve planes and shot down *five* of them before breaking away because he had expended his machine gun ammunition. Unfortunately the fight took place far behind the enemy lines and Putnam received official credit for only three planes. But much later others who claimed they had witnessed this great air battle declared that Putnam had shot down a total of five.

Had Dave Putnam remained in Captain Madon's squadron he might have doubled or even tripled his number of air victories. At that time, however, American volunteer pilots were being released by the French Flying Service so they could transfer to the U.S. Air Service. On June 14 Putnam left French Spad Squadron No. 38 to be commissioned a first lieutenant in the U.S. Air Service and given the command of the 134th Pursuit Squadron.

Those who served with Putnam believed that his responsibilities as commanding officer took some of the edge off his own flying. As an officer he felt it was his main job to watch over those under him instead of roaming the air alone in search of combat, and as a result his fast mounting personal score of enemy victories came to a more or less abrupt halt. Although he probably did shoot down some German planes that were not officially confirmed, it is a matter of record that only one more air victory was officially credited to Putnam before he himself was killed in air battle on September 13, 1918.

There were three or four different stories as to just how Putnam met his death, but the one accepted at the time by most pilots was that while on patrol with one of his pilots behind the German lines, he saw an American two-seater observation plane being attacked by eight German Fokkers. He instantly went to the two-seater's rescue and shot down one of the German planes. At that precise moment, though, fifteen more German planes dropped down on him from out of the sun and eventually sent him hurtling in flames to the ground.

Putnam was buried with full military honors in a cemetery close to the French city of Toul. His grave is located next to the grave of Raoul Lufbery, and somehow it seems quite fitting that those two great aces—both of whose lives ended tragically—should lie side by side in death.

Chapter
TWELVE

When word was flashed around the world on April 6, 1917, that the United States had declared war on Germany, probably no group of Americans was more elated by the news than the pilots of the Lafayette Flying Corps. And shortly afterward when Gen. John J. Pershing arrived in France with the first contingent of American troops, every Lafayette pilot who could go rushed to Paris to cheer himself hoarse at the sight of his countrymen parading in full battle array. Now things would happen, and in a big way, those cheering watchers thought. Soon thousands of American airplanes and pilots would arrive to help the British, the French, and the Lafayette pilots drive the Germans out of the sky completely.

But it was not to be that way at all.

Not long after America entered the war the Executive Committee of the Lafayette Flying Corps held a special meeting in its Paris offices. At the meeting it was decided that the members of the Lafayette Escadrille and all other American volunteer pilots flying in French uniform should be asked if they wished to offer their services to the U.S. Air Service. The decision, yes or no, would be strictly up to each pilot, and he would be under no pressure to make a choice against his will.

It was not an easy decision for any of the pilots. For many months they had been a part of the French Flying Service. They had flown and fought day in and day out with their French flying mates and had formed strong friendships. And in the majority of cases they had come to regard France as a second homeland for which they had almost as much love as for their true one.

No pilot reached his decision overnight. He talked it over with his particular buddy, and the others, too. It was discussed in their sleeping quarters, while waiting to go on patrol, in the mess tents, and at most every other time except when they were in the air on patrol.

In the end the decision to request a transfer to the U.S. Air Service was unanimous, and what tipped the scales was the fact that the French Government made no attempt to hold them to their enlistment pledges. It agreed without any argument to release any American volunteer pilot from the French Flying Service if he so desired. Another thing that caused the pilots to decide to offer their services to the U.S. Air Service was the firm belief that their first duty now was to their own country. So the decision was made—but before the transfer was completed, thirty-three of the American volunteer pilots had changed their minds and elected to remain in the French Flying Service.

Several unfortunate factors brought on this change of mind: delays caused by U.S. Government red tape, the fact that the pilots were practically ignored for months after they had offered their services, and some almost incredible bungling by the brass of the U.S. Air Service in France. Unbelievable as it may seem, the battle-seasoned pilots of the Lafayette Flying Corps were virtually overlooked by the powers that be in Washington, D.C., and the high brass in France until the fall of 1917. And even then many of the American volunteer pilots did not receive their U.S. Air Service commissions until January and February of 1918. The French Flying Service had released them, but the U.S. Air Service had not accepted them yet. Technically they were civilian pilots, although they were still flying with a French squadron and still wearing the French uniform!

It must be stated, however, that there were a few U.S. Air Service officers of high rank in France who realized the value of forming the American air forces around a core of experienced Lafayette pilots. One of the most outspoken was Col. William (Billy) Mitchell. He repeatedly beseeched the War Department in Washington to take over the Lafayette Escadrille as a unit and to form other U.S. Air Service squadrons composed of the Lafayette Flying Corps pilots who were flying with French squadrons. He also suggested that the United States begin immediate manufacture of war planes patterned on existing British and French designs so that yet-to-be-trained U.S. Air Service pilots would have something to fly when they eventually arrived in France. But both of Colonel Mitchell's pleas were ignored.

At that time the top military men in the U.S. Government had their own grand idea of what should be done. Their dream was to build a great U.S. air arm according to their own pattern, and to do it almost overnight. Thousands of American youths would be trained to fly, and thousands of airplanes of strictly American design and manufacture would be supplied to them to fly against the Germans. In time, but *not* overnight, thousands of America's youth were trained as war pilots, but thousands of war planes of American design and manufacture *were never produced*. The planes that American industry finally turned out and shipped to France for the U.S. Air Service were *all* of either French or British design. Not one single airplane of American design ever reached the front in World War I.

The bungling and ofttimes downright stupidity of the U.S.

Air Service high brass in France literally stunned the Lafayette pilots and hurt them deeply. Many of them had been in France for two years; they had risked their lives almost daily, first in trench fighting, then in air fighting. Yet when their own country entered the war and they eagerly offered their services, they were treated as though they had yet to fire a shot in battle. They simply could not understand such treatment, and when the U.S. Air Service finally did agree to take them over, thirty-three shook their heads and said, "No thanks!"

A good example of the almost unbelievable stupidity of the U.S. Air Service brass during the take-over period is conveyed in an incident which took place at the Lafayette Escadrille's Chaudun airfield one day in October, 1917. Five months earlier the American volunteer pilots had offered their services to the U.S. Air Service, but not until that October day did the U.S. Air Service brass do something about them. Air Service doctors were sent to the squadron to give the pilots a medical examination *to determine if they could be accepted.* The report turned in by those examining doctors never became a part of the official U.S. Air Service files, but some of what it contained was made known at the time.

The report stated that in general those examined were physically, mentally, and morally unfit to be pilots! For example, it was found that Dudley Hill had one blind eye, and that Bill Thaw's vision was far below that required of a pilot. If that were not enough to rule out Thaw, he also had a crippled arm. Raoul Lufbery was declared to be so knotted up with rheumatism that he was in constant danger of losing control of his airplane and crashing to his death. Another veteran airman's tonsils were in such terrible condition that he couldn't possibly fly at the front. And still another of the Lafayette Escadrille pilots would be a flying risk *because he had flat feet!*

According to this doctors' report, the world-famous Lafa-

139

yette Escadrille pilots were in utterly hopeless shape and a bad risk all around. Fortunately, that incredible medical report either became lost on its way to the higher-ups, or someone tossed it in the nearest wastebasket. At any rate, Bill Thaw, Raoul Lufbery, and the other "hopeless cripples" continued to fight the air war. As a matter of fact, on the very day of the examination, the pilots of the Lafayette Escadrille made two patrols over the enemy lines and shot down a German plane on each patrol.

The summer and fall months of 1917 proved to be bitterly disappointing ones for the pilots of the Lafayette Flying Corps. Their joy at America's entry into the war faded more and more as they grimly continued to battle the Germans in the high sky, even though they lacked official identity as either French Flying Service or U.S. Air Service pilots. Then at long last, on February 18, 1918, the U.S. Air Service finally took over the Lafayette Flying Corps. The Lafayette Escadrille was made the 103rd U.S. Air Service Pursuit Squadron and the other Lafayette pilots were assigned to various American air squadrons. Some were named commanding officers, and others, flight leaders; but all were given commissions in the U.S. Air Service.

At first it looked to the veteran American volunteer pilots as if everything was finally going to go in their favor, but actually the bungling had only begun.

When the Lafayette Escadrille became the 103rd Pursuit Squadron, Bill Thaw was made a major and given command of the squadron. There were eleven other pilots on the flying roster, and to that number were added six former Lafayette pilots who had been serving with French squadrons. That made the squadron's strength eighteen pilots, all of whom believed, from Bill Thaw on down, that they were going to fly and fight together as a single unit. But that wasn't the way it turned out. Within less than three months, three quarters of the pilots had been reassigned to other American pursuit squadrons. Only a handful of the original Lafayette Squadron pilots remained, and instead of being a fighting squadron, the 103rd Pursuit became simply a training squadron at the front for new pilots. To all intents and purposes, the famed Lafayette Escadrille was no more.

This was a terrific blow to the morale of those few air-war veterans who remained in the squadron, but they refused to let it break them. Their will to fight survived in spite of the shabby treatment they were given, and it is interesting to note that of the forty-four enemy planes the 103rd Pursuit Squadron shot down in World War I, twenty-five were destroyed by that handful of former Lafayette Escadrille pilots.

Perhaps the rawest deal handed to any Lafayette Flying Corps pilot was that which Raoul Lufbery, its ace of aces, suffered.

When Thaw was made a major and put in command of the 103rd Pursuit, Lufbery was promoted to the same rank and put in command of the U.S. Air Service 95th Pursuit Squadron. That would have been fine, except that there was no 95th Pursuit Squadron! At the time it was only a squadron on paper without a single pilot save Lufbery, and not one single airplane to fly.

So instead of going to the front to take over command of an active fighter squadron, Raoul Lufbery went to the American Aviation Instruction Center at Issoudun where he was given a desk job—but with absolutely nothing to do. Day after day he sat at his desk waiting for the so-called 95th Pursuit to be formed, but a month went by and still nothing had happened. Almost every day Lufbery pleaded with the U.S. Air Service high brass to be relieved of his meaningless assignment and returned to front-line action. His superiors turned down his request each time, however, and coldly told him to let them organize the U.S. Air Service.

Raoul Lufbery thought he was finally going to get some action when he was sent with the 95th Pursuit Squadron, which had been formed at last, to Villeneuve on the Champagne front. When he arrived there, though, eager to whip his fledgling pilots into shape and lead them against the Germans, he found only a few old beaten-up Nieuport 27s on the airfield—and not a single one of them armed!

It would have been practically suicide for even Lufbery to fly one of those old Nieuport 27s against the Germans, and outright murder to allow any of his pilots to get within range of German aerial guns. So until machine guns for the planes did arrive, the only thing Lufbery could do was to teach his pilots combat tactics in the safe air over the field. On occasion he would lead them close enough to the lines to get a look at the war on the German side and still be safe from enemy attack. And when he wasn't flying he gave lectures on the best ways to attack certain German planes, or held long question and answer sessions with his pilots.

For Lufbery the situation must have been frustrating and maddening beyond words. Those who knew him at the time said later that it had drastically changed his personality. In the old days as a Lafayette Escadrille pilot he had been an easygoing lover of practical jokes, except when he was in the air, and always seemed to be in the best of spirits. But the poor treatment he received from the U.S. Air Service brass turned him into a man who was moody and morose, one who seldom smiled.

Despite his grievances, however, Raoul Lufbery never for an instant slowed up his efforts to teach his pilots as much as he possibly could, and he spent countless hours in the air with them. He took a special interest in three green American pilots who, he predicted, would make an air-war name for themselves once they got the chance. His prediction came true, for those

142

three pilots were Eddie Rickenbacker, who eventually became the U.S. Air Service's top ace, and Reid Chambers and Douglas Campbell, both of whom set high scores for German planes shot down and confirmed.

Without machine guns for the Nieuports, though, Lufbery could not lead his pilots into battle to receive their trial by fire. As week followed week, and still no machine guns had arrived, Lufbery's spirits sank lower and lower. On one occasion, after he had led some of his pilots on a safe surveillance flight near the front, he fueled up his plane and took off again alone. He flew over to Le Ferme de la Noblette where the 103rd U.S. Air Service Squadron was stationed, and held a reunion with the few old Lafayette Escadrille pilots who were still with the squadron.

As one of the 103rd's pilots reported later, Lufbery talked bitterly of his plight. He pointed out that it had been nearly a year since the United States declared war, but what was he doing? Waiting for aerial machine guns! Six hundred million dollars had been appropriated for the U.S. Air Service, yet all he and his pilots could do was to make practice patrols well behind the Allied lines because they couldn't get aerial machine guns to equip even half a dozen of the beat-up Nieuport 27s. How did anyone expect to win a war that way?

On April 10, wonder of wonders, some aerial machine guns finally did arrive at the 95th Pursuit Squadron—*exactly five of them!* But five aerial machine guns were better than none at all; at least five of the pilots could go into action. Lufbery had the guns installed at once on the five best Nieuports and started leading four of his most skillful pilots across the front lines. It so happened, though, that air activity on that particular front had slowed down considerably, and only now and then did Lufbery and his young American pilots spot a German plane. Just the same the patrols into German-held air were valuable experiences for the beginners and they learned many things which were to help them later when they were assigned to more active fronts.

For Lufbery, though, it was frustrating to try to conduct an air war at only about one quarter strength. Quite often when he had brought a patrol safely back from the front lines, he would take off again alone to fly deep into German-held air in search of battle, as he had so often done in his Lafayette Escadrille days. But on those lone-wolf flights his old luck seemed to have left him, for not once was he able to fight an air duel with a German pilot. Time after time he would spot an enemy plane, only to see it turn tail a moment later and streak for safety before he could get close enough to attack.

Then came May 19, 1918, and a tragic end for Raoul Lufbery, the Lafayette's ace of aces.

It was about midmorning, so the story goes, when a lone German Albatros two-seater observation plane appeared in the high sky over the 95th Squadron's airfield. A few moments later French aircraft batteries opened fire on it. Suddenly the German plane fell off on one wing as though struck by one of the exploding antiaircraft shells. It started spinning downward, but when it was only a few thousand feet above the ground, it came out of the spin and banked around east to go limping toward the German side of the lines.

Lufbery was one of those who happened to be on the airfield and saw the Albatros spin down, then recover and head for home. It looked like an easy victory for him, and he leaped into the nearest Nieuport, his own being in repairs at the time, and went racing off the ground in pursuit of the Albatros. Since the Nieuport was miles faster than the Albatros, Lufbery soon caught up with it, and those watching saw him fire several bursts of machine gun bullets. Nothing happened, though, and the German plane continued to fly eastward. Apparently the

144

two cockpits on the enemy plane were protected by armor, because Lufbery was too expert a shot to have missed.

Pulling out of his dive and gaining some altitude, Lufbery attacked again, but suddenly veered off. Probably his gun had jammed and he wanted to get some distance from the German plane while he cleared it. After a few moments those on the ground watching saw Lufbery go for the Albatros a third time, but this time from the rear. Exactly what happened next, no one was able to tell for sure. Perhaps Lufbery fired his gun or perhaps he didn't, but the German observer in the rear cockpit of the Albatros must have fired his gun because the Nieuport suddenly burst into flames.

For a moment or two it staggered through the air, then it went side-slipping downward toward the earth. When the plane reached a very low altitude it seemed to level off, and those watching in horror saw Lufbery climb out of the cockpit and jump. He fell in the back yard of a peasant woman's cottage, and when his comrades arrived at the spot they found her covering the body with flowers. His funeral took place the next day and he was buried in the cemetery near Toul where that other great Lafayette ace, Dave Putnam, was to join him four months later.

Lufbery's flying mates asked themselves over and over why he had jumped from his burning plane, but they could never be certain of the answer. Several of the pilots remembered that he had always had a great fear of fire in the air and had declared that if his plane ever caught fire he would jump rather than suffer the agony of a flaming death. These pilots guessed that Lufbery, after failing to blow out the fire by side-slipping the Nieuport down through the air, had seen no other course but to jump.

Others who had flown with him, though, claimed he had no such morbid fear of fire in the air. In their opinion, Lufbery had not jumped because of the flames, but because his plane was over a small river and he hoped he would land in the water and somehow save his life. Instead, he had misjudged the jump and fallen to earth in the peasant woman's back yard.

Whatever their view of the accident itself, however, many who had served with Lufbery couldn't help wondering if the disappointment, frustration, and despair he had suffered after putting on the uniform of the U.S. Air Service had slowly robbed him of his confidence as a pilot. And perhaps it was this loss, more than anything else, which in the end cost him his life while doing battle with just a single slow-moving German airplane.

Chapter
THIRTEEN

When the Lafayette Escadrille became the 103rd U.S. Air Service Pursuit Squadron on February 18, 1918, and other Lafayette pilots became members of other U.S. Air Service squadrons, it marked the end of a chapter of air-war history. Although the Lafayette men continued to fly and fight in the high skies, it was never the same for them again. No longer were they a volunteer group bound to each other by an unusually strong esprit de corps. Instead, they became just so many fighter pilots scattered throughout the war zone, and the name Lafayette disappeared from army orders and citations.

There was still a war to be won, however, and every Lafayette pilot continued to give all he had to the struggle for control of the skies. In spite of the often unfair and unwarranted treatment they received, none of them ever lost sight of the cause for which they were fighting. They had been involved in the war too long, and had too much at stake, to allow any lessening of their efforts.

No story of the Lafayette Flying Corps would be complete without mention of and praise for the four French officers who commanded the Lafayette Escadrille between April 20, 1916, when it was initiated, and February 18, 1918, when it became the 103rd U.S. Air Service Pursuit Squadron.

In all the French armed forces in World War I, it is unlikely that any officer earned more respect and admiration from the men serving under him than Capt. Georges Thénault. He was not only the Lafayette squadron's commander throughout its entire existence, but also a friend of each of the pilots.

Captain Thénault wore the uniform of the French Flying Service from the day the war started to the day it ended. A crack air pilot and a born leader of men, Thénault also possessed the admirable quality of being able to delegate leadership authority to others and obtain satisfactory results. A splendid example was his selection of Lt. Alfred de Laage de Meux as adjutant and second in command of the *Escadrille Américaine*.

Another veteran of the war from the very beginning, Lt. de Laage de Meux was serving as a second lieutenant in the French 14th Regiment of Dragoons on the day war broke out, and was immediately assigned to front-line duty. Once when he was out on a reconnoitering patrol his horse was shot out from under him and he himself was wounded in the leg. By good fortune his orderly, Jean Dressy, who was later to follow him into the French Flying Service, had accompanied him on the patrol and was able to carry the wounded officer back to safety before German cavalry could arrive to take them both prisoner.

In March of 1915 Lt. de Laage de Meux obtained his transfer to the French Flying Service and was assigned to a French Caudron squadron as an observer. His great desire, though, was to become a pilot and he requested assignment to a flying school. The request was denied so vehemently that he never made a second one. Instead, he learned to fly on his own at the front when he wasn't busy performing his duties as the ob-

149

server and rear gunner on a Caudron observation plane. By so doing he became one of the few pilots in the French Flying Service who had never attended a flight training school.

Not long after Lt. de Laage de Meux learned to fly he was sent as a pilot to another French observation squadron that was flying the prewar Farman biplane. Shortly after his arrival he shot down his first German plane, and because of the piloting ability he displayed every time he was in the air, he was soon transferred to a French pursuit squadron. So daring was his flying and so apparently contemptuous was he of danger in the air that his superiors gloomily predicted he would meet an early death. He fooled them all, even though more than once he brought his plane back from patrol so badly shot up that no one could understand how he had managed to keep it in the air.

When Captain Thénault was given command of the *Escadrille Américaine,* he happened to meet Lt. de Laage de Meux and was so impressed by him that he asked his superiors to assign the daring pilot to the newly formed all-American air squadron as its adjutant and second in command. The transfer assignment was made, and starting with the first day of his new duties, Lt. de Laage de Meux became more and more of a favorite with the American volunteer pilots. To them he typified a Frenchman of culture, as well as being a man of almost irresistible personal charm.

Lt. de Laage de Meux was killed on May 23, 1917, but not while fighting Germans in the sky over No Man's Land. He died as the result of one of those hard-luck accidents that could happen to the best of pilots. On the afternoon of that day he was taking off to go on patrol, and as usual he held the airplane on the ground as long as he could to let the engine develop maximum horsepower. Then he intended to pull the plane off the ground as he always did, and send it prop-clawing up in a climbing turn for altitude.

But this time the engine of his Spad suddenly quit cold on him. Before he could level off from the climb, the heavy plane stalled and fell into a spin. Since it was so close to the ground, Lt. de Laage de Meux couldn't recover from the spin and regain flying speed, and the Spad spun down into the ground, killing him instantly.

The French officer who took Lt. de Laage de Meux's place as second in command of the Lafayette Escadrille was Lt. Antoine Arnoux de Maison Rouge. For him the job must have been extremely difficult at the start because the pilots were still mourning their beloved Lieutenant de Laage and unconsciously showed a resentment of the man taking his place. Arnoux was, however, a man of great tact and understanding. He did his job so quietly and in such a friendly spirit that in no time the pilots buried any resentment they may have felt and began to show a liking for the man.

Like Lt. de Laage de Meux, Lieutenant Arnoux had been serving in the French cavalry when war broke out, and he had seen immediate action. He continued to serve with his cavalry unit until the middle of 1915, when cavalry as a weapon of war was abolished. He then enlisted in the French Flying Service and was breveted a pilot on the Maurice Farman observation plane in November of that year. He served with a French Nieuport squadron until May 28, 1917, when he joined the Lafayette Escadrille as its second in command.

Lieutenant Arnoux was an excellent combat pilot and a skillful patrol leader, and he soon won the high admiration of every pilot in the squadron. Because he repeatedly took on new jobs rather than turn them over to one of his pilots, Arnoux de Maison Rouge eventually taxed his strength beyond the limit. In early October, 1917, he became seriously ill and was forced to go to the rear to rest and recuperate. A month later he returned to the front, but for duty with another French Spad squadron, No. 78. In May, 1918, he took on one more German plane than he could handle, and after a terrific air battle he was shot down in flames far behind the German lines.

The third and last French officer to become second in command of the Lafayette Escadrille was Lt. Louis Verdier-Fauvety. He, too, had served in the French cavalry at the start of the war, and in February of 1916 he also enlisted in the French Flying Service. He went to the front in October of that year to serve with the famous French Escadrille N. 65, which boasted the great Nungesser on its roster of pilots.

During his time with the French squadron, he had had an experience in the air which resulted in one of the most miraculous escapes from death in the entire war. One day while flying at an altitude of twelve thousand feet, Lieutenant Verdier-Fauvety collided with another Spad and his plane's stabilizer was torn off. The right wings of the other pilot's plane were ripped off, and he fell instantly to his death. Lieutenant Verdier-Fauvety's Spad also went plunging out of control toward earth and crashed in some woods, but by some miracle he received only a few minor injuries from the 12,000-foot fall!

Lieutenant Verdier-Fauvety served with Nungesser's squadron until October 6, 1917, when he joined the Lafayette Escadrille as its new second in command. He fitted into his new job with no trouble at all and was soon accepted by the American volunteer pilots with the same warmth and affection they had shown his two predecessors. When the U.S. Air Service took over the Lafayette Escadrille and Lieutenant Verdier-Fauvety left it to join another French pursuit squadron, all the American pilots were sorry to see him go.

Incidentally, Lieutenant Verdier-Fauvety returned to the same French pursuit squadron he had served with before joining the Lafayette Escadrille, and a short time later he was made its commanding officer. But he was not destined to fly and fight for France much longer. On August 21, 1918, after almost four years of continuous service on various war fronts, Lieutenant

Verdier-Fauvety was killed during a German night bombing attack on his airfield.

When World War I ended on November 11, 1918, a total of 267 American volunteers had originally enlisted in the French Flying Service. Of that number, 180 saw combat service on the fighting fronts, 43 were released for various reasons before obtaining their wings, 5 died of illness, and 6 were killed in flight training school accidents. The remaining 33 of the 267 total were still in flight training when the U.S. Air Service took over the Lafayette Flying Corps.

Of the 180 who actually saw service on the fighting fronts, 38 served in the Lafayette Escadrille, and the other 142 saw service with some 65 different French Pursuit squadrons and 27 observation and bombing squadrons. Altogether the group shot down 199 officially confirmed enemy planes (better than one plane per man) and undoubtedly twice that number of enemy planes which were not officially confirmed. The price the Lafayette boys paid for that splendid record was 55 pilots killed in action, 19 wounded, and 15 taken prisoner. But three of the pilots forced down and captured by the Germans managed later to escape and return to the Allied side of the lines for more combat duty. And when the United States entered the war, 93 of the Lafayette pilots transferred to the U.S. Air Service, 26 transferred to U.S. Naval Aviation, and 33 continued to fly with French Air Squadrons.

Those in brief summary are the cold statistics of the Lafayette Flying Corps, whose record of achievement will live forever in air-war history. But, in a sense, the fine work of the Corps did not stop when its pilots were taken over by the U.S. Air Service, nor even when the war ended. The bitter lessons these pilots had learned, and the hard-won knowledge of aerial combat that they had gained, were to serve as guides in the long-range planning of American military aviation after the war.

The start of World War I saw the birth of the airplane as a weapon of war; by the time the conflict ended it had become one of the most potentially destructive weapons of all. At first, though, the perfecting and mastering of aerial warfare techniques was a matter of trial and error. Both sides started from scratch, and what the early pilots learned was passed along to those who followed them. The early French pilots instructed the Lafayette pilots, who in turn passed along their knowledge of successful aerial warfare to the fledgling American fliers placed under their command after the Corps was taken over by the U.S. Air Service. As a matter of fact, many of the air fighting tactics the Lafayette pilots had perfected in actual combat, and taught to the greenhorn American pilots assigned to them, were to become future standard practices for U.S. Air Service pilots taking combat training.

Another far-reaching and lasting contribution made by those gallant Lafayette Flying Corps pilots was the inspiration they gave to American youth, encouraging them to become airminded. Stories of the Corps pilots' aerial feats in French skies stirred thousands of American boys back home, and filled them with the desire to follow in the footsteps of their heroes. Many accomplished this while World War I was still raging, and those who were too young at the time clung to their dream until years later when they could make it come true in the expanding U.S. Air Force.

The pilots of the Lafayette Flying Corps pioneered the way for other young Americans not only in time of war, but in time of peace as well. In a sense they did much to awaken American youth to the great challenge of the airplane, and eventually that challenge was picked up by men like Charles Lindbergh, Richard Byrd, Clarence Chamberlain, Frank Hawks, Wiley Post, and a host of other peacetime air greats who did their full share to help win a leading place for American aviation on the world scene.

And although it may be overlooked in the wake of more dramatic consequences, the Lafayette Flying Corps also made a sizable payment on America's long-standing debt to France's gallant Marquis de Lafayette, that ardent supporter of our young country at a time when it needed friends even more desperately than his native France needed them in World War I.

For Further Reading

While most of these titles are not chiefly concerned with military aviation in World War I, they all provide interesting and helpful background information on the War, on why and how it was fought, and on the men who did the fighting—both on the ground and in the air.

Castor, Henry, *America's First World War: General Pershing and the Yanks.* New York: Random House, 1957.

Colby, C. B., *Fighting Gear of World War I.* New York: Coward-McCann, 1961.

Cowley, Robert, *1918:Gamble for Victory; the Greatest Attack of World War I.* New York: Macmillan, 1964.

Editors of the "Army Times," *Famous Fighters of World War I.* New York: Dodd, Mead & Company, 1964.

Nordhoff, Charles, *Falcons of France: A Tale of Youth and the Air.* Boston: Little, Brown & Company, 1929.

Reeder, Col. Red, *The Story of the First World War.* New York: Duell, Sloan, and Pearce, 1962.

Sellman, R. R., *The First World War.* New York: Criterion Books, 1962.

Snyder, Louis L., *The First Book of World War I.* New York: Franklin Watts, 1958.

Index

17s compared with 27s, 79; fuel supply of, 91; Lafayette Escadrille changes over from, 113-14, 117; for 95th Pursuit Squadron, 142-44

Night flying, 93, 101, 102-6

Nungesser, Lieutenant Charles, 50, 51

Parachutes, lack of, 48

Parsons, Edwin C. ("Ted"), 122, 129; joins French Flying Service, 115-16; poor health of, 115; remains in French service, 116

Pau flying school, 18, 34, 45, 126; all American volunteers assigned to training at, 35-36, 37

Pavelka, Paul: close escapes of, 101-6; death of, 106

Pourpe, Marc: Lufbery and, 55-56

Prince, Frederick H., 96

Prince, Norman, 63, 71, 75; conceives idea for all-American squadron, 32-33, 34-35; assigned to front, 36; on leave in U.S., 36-37; at Le Bourget school, 37; as original member of *Escadrille Américaine*, 39, 40; promoted, 41; victories of, 76, 87; captures German airplane, 83-86; last mission of, 90, 92-95

Putnam, David, 130-35; number of victories of, 125; killed, 134-35

Rickenbacker, Edward, 143

Rockwell, Kiffin, 63; volunteers for French Army, 44-45; as original member of *Escadrille Américaine*, 39, 40, 41; first victory of, 45-48, 49; shot down, 80-83

Rumsey, Lawrence, joins *Escadrille Américaine*, 52

Russian front, supposed first aerial warfare on, 6-7

Saint Just, Lafayette Escadrille at, 113, 114-24

Sinclaire, Reginald, 129

Soubiran, Robert: in Foreign Legion, 96; joins *Escadrille Américaine*, 97; transfers to U.S. Air Service, 97-98

Spads: described, 113-14; Lafayette Escadrille changes over to, 113-14, 117; as "Flying Brick," 128

Spies: landed by Bach, 22-26; in French Flying Service, 27-28

Thaw, William, 98, 106, 114, 116; in Foreign Legion, 27-29; transfers to Flying Service, 29-32; assigned to front, 35-36, 37; on leave in U.S., 36-37; as original member of *Escadrille Américaine*, 39, 40; promoted, 41; scores a victory, 50-51; wounded, 58-59; suggests "Lafayette Escadrille," 109; supposed disabilities of, 139, 140; commands 103rd Pursuit Squadron, 140

Thénault, Captain Georges, 51, 63, 69; as commander of *Escadrille Américaine*, 40, 149; training policy of, 41-42, 49; leads squadron on first mission 42-44; in German trap, 71-75

U.S. Air Service: transfer from Lafayette Flying Corps to, 116, 136-40, 154; bungling in, 138-40; contribution of Lafayette Flying Corps to, 155

U.S. 95th Pursuit Squadron, Lufbery and, 141-44

U.S. 103rd Pursuit Squadron, 114, 116, 143; established from Lafayette Escadrille, 140-41; Thaw as commanding officer of, 140; Soubiran as commanding officer of, 97; combat record of, 141

U.S. 134th Pursuit Squadron, 134

U.S. Naval Aviation, 154

Vanderbilt, William K., 34, 111

Verdier-Fauvety, Lieutenant Louis, 152-53

Whiskey (mascot), 76-77, 113